"After This"

"AFTER THIS"

Or

The Church, The Kingdom, and The Glory

By
PHILIP MAURO

"And to this agree the words of the prophets as it is written, *After This I Will Return*, and will build again the Tabernacle of David which is fallen down" (Acts 15 : 15, 16)

NEW YORK CHICAGO

Fleming H. Revell Company

LONDON AND EDINBURGH

1917

Printed in the United States of America

New York: 158 Fifth Avenue
Chicago: 17 North Wabash Ave.
London: 21 Paternoster Square
Edinburgh: 75 Princes Street

Preface

GOD has been pleased to make known in His Word what will happen "after this"; and surely there should be the liveliest interest in the subject of earth's future, especially in the present era of unprecedented "destruction and misery," in which human progress and civilization have eventuated. Who is there that would not give much to be informed, from a sure and trustworthy source, just what will happen "after this"? And that information, from Him Who has planned all things from the foundation of the world, is within the reach of those who are willing to give heed to the "more sure word of prophecy."

"After this *I* will return," is the sure promise of One Who cannot lie and Who will not fail. His return is that for which creation itself waits and "groans." Once He came to earth in lowly guise; and even then the works and powers of darkness fled away from His presence, while peace, healing, safety and blessing attended the path of His feet. For God had anointed Him "with the Holy Ghost and with power; Who went about doing good and healing all that were oppressed of the devil." We have in His own words the record of the effects of His presence, as He said: "The blind receive their sight, and the lame walk, the lepers are cleansed, and the deaf hear, the dead are raised up, and the poor have the Gospel preached unto them" (Matt. 11:5).

But the world wished not to receive Him; His citizens hated Him and said: "We will not have this Man to reign over us." So "they caught Him, and cast Him out of the vineyard and slew Him." Hence it is decreed of God that, since *earth* despised and rejected Him, "the *heaven* must receive Him until the times of restitution of all things, which God hath spoken by the mouth of all His holy prophets since the world began" (Acts 3:21). In those promised "times of restitution," which now are close at hand, conditions throughout the entire world will be what they were on a very small scale in His immediate presence when He was upon earth the first time. For those will be "times of *refreshing*,"—that is, of reviving, revitalizing, rejuvenating, reinvigorating, of all creation, mankind especially—"from the *presence* of the Lord" (Acts 3:19).

Meanwhile, the earth is left in the hands of men. God has given them freedom and every opportunity to try all their experiments, to develop all their schemes of world-building, to prove the worth of all their scientific discoveries, political theories, and the like, without check or hindrance from Him Who is "Lord of all." For, in the majestic unfolding of God's "plan of the ages, which He purposed in Christ Jesus our Lord" (Eph. 3:11, Gr.), it was from the very beginning arranged that the "times of *refreshing*" and of "*restitution*" should be preceded by "the times of the GENTILES" (Luke 21:24).

In order that the need of the government of GOD'S

King (Psa. 2:6) may be fully manifested, time is granted for the trying out of all systems of *human* government, down to the very last of all—the extremities represented by the feet and toes of Nebuchadnezzar's image (Dan. 2:41–45). For when we come to the "toes of the feet," we reach the *very end* of man's political or governmental line of things. And since that is the stage at which "the God of heaven shall set up a kingdom which shall never be destroyed," it is easy to find in the vision of the first Gentile world-ruler, as in many other Scriptures, a clear indication of the extent and limit of that period which is designated by the words, "after this."

Our present purpose is to examine, in the clear light of Scripture, that marvellously interesting age in which we are living—"this present evil age" (Gal. 1:4)—with the definite object of learning *just what part of God's vast purpose* has been assigned to this period of time. When we have become acquainted (as is comparatively easy to do, and is well worth a hundred times the effort required to that end) with the special things which God has planned to accomplish in this age of the Lord's rejection and absence, we will be able to approximate, with all necessary exactness, the time of the Lord's coming again. For He has said, "After THIS I will return."

For, just as the sufferings and death of Christ "must needs" have taken place ere the foreordained work of this age could be even begun, that is, before the Gospel could be preached "with the Holy Ghost sent down from heaven" (see John 7:39), even so "must" that foreordained work of "visiting the Gentiles" be fully consummated ere "the times of the Gentiles" be ended and "the times of refreshing from the presence of the Lord" be ushered in.

One remarkable and deeply interesting feature of "this present age" is that *it did not come into the line of vision of the Old Testament prophets.* This age, and the things it contains, were always a fixed and a necessary part of God's eternal plan, but they had been "*kept secret* from the foundation of the world" (Matt. 13:35; Rom. 16:25; Eph. 3:5). The prophets of old foresaw the coming of Christ, His humiliation, rejection, betrayal and death; and they foresaw also His glorious reign over all the nations of earth, with repentant Israel (gathered and restored) in the place of supremacy. But, notwithstanding they "inquired and searched diligently," it was not given them to know "what, or *what manner of time* the Spirit of Christ which was in them did signify, when He testified beforehand the *sufferings* of Christ and the *glories* which should follow" (1 Pet. 1:10–12).

To the redeemed people of God in this age, who have "turned to God from idols to serve the living and true God and to *wait for His Son from heaven*"—(1 Thess. 1:9, 10), is "given" the wonderful privilege of knowing the marvellously interesting things—"which things the angels desire to look into"—that were hidden from the prophets and righteous men of old. How much do we esteem and value that privilege? And what effort are we willing to make in order to profit by it? Are we but languidly interested, or perhaps not at all, in things which prophets and righteous men diligently inquired of, and which "the angels desire to look into"? Let us cast off such indifference, and give the more earnest heed to the things "which," says Peter, "are now reported unto you by them that have preached the Gospel to you with the Holy Ghost sent down from heaven."

Because of the fact that this present age and the things pertaining to it were hidden in the secret counsels of God prior to the first coming of Christ, they are termed "mysteries," that is to say, *divine secrets.* But now the Lord Himself, by His own words and also through His apostles—notably by Paul—has "revealed" those secrets. Hence, to those who have "the revelation of the mystery" (Rom. 16:26), they are not secrets or "mysteries" any longer.

The leading feature of God's great work for this age is the introduction into the world of *"the Kingdom of heaven,"* which is the prominent subject of the New Testament. Hence, the "mysteries" of this age are "the mysteries of the Kingdom of heaven"; that is to say, they have to do with that Kingdom. Therefore it is *absolutely essential* to a right understanding of this present age, and its place in God's vast plan, to know with certainty *what* the Kingdom of heaven is, *where* it is, and *when;* to know its beginning and ending, and who are in it and who are without. To be mistaken about these matters is to be astray as to God's plan in its entirety. Unhappily, many expositors of Scripture, some of whom are highly gifted, have, in their teaching, displaced the "*Kingdom of heaven*" from its proper position in God's plan, removing it from this present age, where it belongs (and always has belonged) and thus have caused confusion and other regrettable results. Nevertheless, the Word of God in regard to all matters connected with the Kingdom of heaven is so clear and intelligible that any and all believers, who are willing to attend to the instruction which the Scriptures contain, can have full and assured understanding of these important subjects. To that end, our present aim is—not to advance any debatable views or doubtful expositions of Scripture but—simply to bring to the attention of our readers the plain and clear statements of God's own Word. With those statements before one's mind, it is easy to see what the Kingdom of heaven is, and what place it occupies in God's plan of the ages.

P. M.

Burlington, Ia.,

Contents

I

"LO, I COME . . . IT IS WRITTEN OF ME"

WHAT gives to the Scriptures their all-surpassing value to men is that they contain "the knowledge of the Son of God." From the Scriptures, and from them alone, comes the knowledge of Him Whose goings forth are from of old, from everlasting; Whose coming for the redemption of a lost world has been awaited from the beginning.

The Lord Jesus Christ declared the character and purpose of the Scriptures when He said: "They are they which *testify of Me*" (John 5:39); and He made known the object for which they were given when, in talking with two of His disciples, "He expounded unto them in all the Scriptures *the things concerning* HIMSELF" (Luke 24:27). The Scriptures whereof He spoke were the Old Testament; and the chief point of the testimony of the Old Testament was the promise of Christ's coming into the world.

The promise of the coming "Seed of the woman" that was to bruise the serpent's head appears at the very beginning of the Bible (Gen. 3:15). That original promise also tells that the coming Seed should Himself suffer; for the serpent was to "bruise His heel." Thus the very first of all the prophecies concerning Christ is in *two parts.* That is a fact of much significance, as will be seen later on.

All of God's dealings with the world in Old Testament times were in preparation for the coming of that promised "Seed." The purpose of God to send His own Son into the world, as a Man among men, and for the work of redemption, is kept steadily in view in the Old Testament Scriptures. Thus, one particular line of descent from father to son is carefully traced from Adam down. That line might have taken any one of a million and more directions: but the course it took aimed, from the beginning, at *one definite point* in far-off time. For about four thousand years its unbroken course was traced, where every other line of descent (though of mighty kings and conquerors) was lost, until "in the fullness of time" its end was reached in a cattle-shed in Bethlehem of Judah, where a virgin gave birth to a Son. Thus the Seed of the *woman* came into the world which He had created; and He came to do a work that is far greater and costlier than that of creation. In the humble birth of the virgin's Son that long line of descent reached its end, after having pursued for thousands of years a course known only to Him Who sees the end from the beginning—a course that took unexpected and unlikely turns—often passing by the eldest son, and notably, in the case of Jesse's family, a whole series of seven elder sons (1 Sam. 16:6–12); a course that is carefully traced through the centuries before the flood, which did not blot out this genealogy; that traversed other centuries of wanderings in Canaan, of slavery and degradation in Egypt, of struggles for the possession of the promised land, of departures from God and of gross apostasy under the kings, of captivity in Babylon, and of ages of Gentile domination;—never being lost, never turning aside, but ever reaching on toward the promised goal.

And at length, with the birth of the Babe of Bethlehem, the line abruptly stops, for its purpose has been fully accomplished. It has led to the "Book of the Generation of Jesus Christ, the Son of David, the Son of Abraham" (Matt. 1:1). That is the book of *life,* the book of the "New Man."

In the "Book of the Generations of Adam," the first man (Gen. 5), the brief history of each individual closes thus: "and he died." But the history of the "Second Man, the Lord from heaven," does not read in that way. Here we have, in the new book which God now opens, the history—not of one who lived and *died,* but of One Who died and *lived,* and Whose power and influence in the world (far exceeding all other influences put together) are exerted *after* death. This is the history, not of one who brought sin and death into a perfect creation, but of One Who brought righteousness and life into a ruined world (Rom. 5:12–21). This is the account He gives of Himself: "I am He that liveth, and was dead, and, behold, I am alive forevermore, Amen; and have the keys of hell and of death" (Rev. 1:18). Having the keys of hell and of death, He can deliver the captives of Satan. The long foretold "purpose and grace of God" are "now made manifest by the appearing of our Saviour

Jesus Christ, Who hath abolished death and brought life and immortality to light through the Gospel" (2 Tim. 1:9, 10). Therefore, as the One Who "both died, and rose, and revived, that He might be Lord both of the dead and living" (Rom. 14:9), He is preached in all the world to the end that all who hear the gospel of His death and resurrection, and who believe on Him, may not perish but have everlasting life. Those who believe on Him are not written in the book of Adam, who lived and died; but in the book of Jesus Christ, Who died and Who lives again in "the power of an endless life."

Hence God's call to all men now is a call to "repentance toward God and faith toward our Lord Jesus Christ" (Acts 20:21). For He "*now* commandeth all men everywhere to *repent*" (Acts 17:30). May every reader be sure that he has given heed in his heart to this world-wide call of God, Who wills not that any "should perish, but that all should come to repentance" (2 Pet. 3:9).

The important thing to note, for our present purposes, is that the first Coming of Christ into the world (as a Babe born of woman, but without human father), and all that He did while in the world, was strictly in fulfillment of *what was written.* Again and again we read in the Gospels: "Now all this was done, that it might be fulfilled which was spoken of the Lord by the prophet;" "then was fulfilled that which was spoken by Jeremy the prophet," "that it might be fulfilled which was spoken by the prophets."

Thus we learn that all the events of the Lord's

brief human life were not only planned beforehand, but they were foretold by the prophets. The predictions concerning Christ go into minute details, such as His going down into Egypt, His entering Jerusalem on an ass' colt, the piercing of His hands and feet, the words He should speak and that should be spoken to Him while He hung on the cross; thus making it impossible that the One Who should "suffer these things" should be other than the Christ of God.

And we should note that the very first prophecy of the promised Seed of the woman gives just two details concerning His coming—first, that He should bruise the serpent's head, and second, that the serpent should bruise His heel.

The unfolding of each of these earliest predictions would fill volumes. But what we wish to point out is the fact that that first of all prophecies contains *two* distinct things, or groups of events, very different (indeed quite opposite) to each other in character. These two predictions become, in later Scriptures, two distinct and contrasted lines of prophecy. Let us carefully note their general character; for we have here, *at the very beginning of prophecy,* the indication of the first and second comings of Christ.

(1) The bruising of the serpent's head is easily seen in all those later prophecies which speak of the overthrow of the power and dominion of evil and the establishment on earth of a universal kingdom of righteousness and peace. The "head" stands for rule, authority and dominion; and it is the serpent's

head that was to be bruised. The devil has the power of death (Heb. 2:15); he is "the prince of the power of the air" (Eph. 2:2), the "god of this age" (2 Cor. 4:4), the "prince of this world" (John 14:30), and he commands hosts of spiritual wickedness in heavenly places (Eph. 6:12; Rev. 12:7). Thus, the first of all prophecies contains the promise of the overthrow of all the despotic power of the evil one, whose rule has held the world in cruel bondage, and who has filled it with corruption, violence, destruction and misery. Subsequent prophecies extend this promise by bringing into view the Kingdom of God, whereof many and glorious details are given. The passages of Scripture that foretell the reign of the Son of God on earth are voluminous.

(2) The prediction that the serpent should bruise the *heel* of the Coming One had its fulfillment in the crucifixion of the Lord Jesus Christ. His "heel" evidently stands for the "body of flesh" that was "prepared" for Him (Col. 2:11; Heb. 10:5), in which He offered the one and all-sufficient sacrifice for sins, bearing His people's sins in His own body on the tree (1 Pet. 2:24). That body was made "in the *likeness* of *sinful flesh*" (Rom. 8:3); for He took the form of a bond-slave (Phil. 2:7). Hence the appropriateness of the prophetic word-symbol "heel." In that lowly guise, without attractive form nor comeliness, and with no beauty which could be seen, "it pleased the Lord to *bruise* Him" (Isa. 53).

That the betrayal of Christ was brought about by Satan is distinctly stated in the Gospels. First

Satan put into Judas Iscariot's heart to betray the Lord (John 13:2) and then Satan "entered into him" (John 13:27), and used him as the instrument of the betrayal.

The prophecies that relate to the bruising of Christ's heel were *all fulfilled at the Lord's first coming.* The Scriptures make it perfectly clear that *all* the prophecies of that class were fulfilled then. For example, the Apostle Paul declared, in his address in Antioch of Pisidia, that the Jews had "fulfilled" the prophets in condemning Christ, saying: "And when they had *fulfilled all* that was written of Him, they took Him down from the tree, and laid Him in a sepulchre. But God raised Him from the dead" (Acts 13:27–30).

When the Lord was betrayed and the armed multitude came with Judas to take Him in the garden, and when Peter drew sword in His defense, Christ referred to the fact that He could summon legions of angels to His aid, "But how then," He said, "shall the Scriptures be fulfilled that thus it *must* be?" (Matt. 26:54).

And after His resurrection, when the two disciples on their way to Emmaus had spoken of how their rulers had delivered Him to be condemned to death, and had crucified Him, He referred them to the prophets, and said: *"Ought not* the Christ to have *suffered* these things, and to enter into His glory? And beginning at Moses, and *all* the prophets, He expounded unto them in *all* the Scriptures, the things concerning Himself" (Luke 24:19–27). And a little later, He declared to His disciples "that *all things* must be fulfilled, which were written in the law of Moses, and in the prophets, and in the psalms concerning Me." And further He reminded them that: "Thus it is written, and thus it behoved (*i. e.*, was *necessary* for) the Christ to suffer, and to rise from the dead the third day" (Luke 24:44–46).

From these statements of the Lord and the Apostles we learn that no word of the Lord in the Old Testament Scriptures can fall to the ground; and we learn also that everything written of Him *must* have a *literal* fulfillment.

The two distinct classes of prophecies concerning Christ, to which we have referred, are distinguished in the New Testament as the (1) *"sufferings"* and (2) the *"glory"*; and those inspired titles are very useful. Thus Peter, in his first Epistle, when writing of the salvation that is ready to be revealed "at the appearing of Jesus Christ," *i. e.*, when He shall come the second time, points out that the prophets had inquired and searched diligently, greatly desiring to understand *"what*, and *what manner of time* the Spirit of Christ which was in them did signify when He testified beforehand *the sufferings* of Christ, and *the glory* that should follow" (1 Pet. 1:5–12).

This shows that the Old Testament does not reveal the *time* when the two classes of prophecies, (1) the sufferings of Christ, and (2) the glory of Christ, should be fulfilled. In the light of the Old Testament prophecies, it could not be discerned that the prophecies concerning the sufferings of Christ were to be fulfilled at His first coming, and that then, after a long interval, He would come again "in glory." Even the prophets themselves did not know the time of these things. But the New Testament supplies that important information, as we shall endeavor to show. Already it has been made evident, by the Scriptures we have referred to, that "all" the prophecies concerning the *sufferings* of Christ, down to the very last and smallest detail, were "fulfilled" at His first coming. Moreover, the whole of the New Testament history, as contained in the Gospels, shows that *not one* of the many predictions concerning "the *glory* that should follow" was then fulfilled. Just one glimpse of the manner of the yet future "Kingdom of the Son of man" was given to three of the disciples at the Transfiguration (Matt. 16:28; 17:1–9). Peter, referring to that great scene, says: "we were eye-witnesses of His majesty" (2 Pet. 1:16–18). And John says: "We beheld His glory, the glory as of the Only-begotten of the Father" (John 1:14).

The separation, therefore, between the two classes of predictions, is complete. The one class is now wholly fulfilled. The other class *awaits fulfillment.* One part or division of the first prophecy, "thou shalt bruise His heel," has been accomplished. The Lord's words on the cross: "It is finished," proclaimed that great fact. But the serpent's head has not yet been bruised. Satan's authority over the world has not been destroyed. He still blinds the minds of the unbelieving, deceives the nations, keeps the greater part of the world in heathen darkness, plunges the civilized and Christianized nations into the bloodiest of all wars, and manifests "the power of death" on a scale more imposing than ever in the past. Hence the wonderful promises, so many and so great, concerning "the Kingdom of our God and the power of His Christ" (Rev. 12:10), when the "accuser" shall be "cast down," still await their fulfillment.

But the New Testament now gives us information which the Old Testament withheld. For it tells us clearly not only "what" the Spirit signified, but also "what manner of *time*" He signified, when He spake beforehand concerning the *glory* of Christ, which was to "follow" the sufferings.

This information, which God has now given, concerning the *time* and *manner* of the coming glories of Christ in His Kingdom, we purpose to put before our readers in the following pages.

II

"YESTERDAY, TO-DAY, AND FOREVER"

KNOWING, as we now do, that all the prophecies concerning the sufferings of Christ were fulfilled at His first coming, we are able to distinguish, with certainty, the prophecies which are yet to be fulfilled in the future. Hence we are in an advantageous position to pursue our inquiries profitably.

Moreover, the records of the New Testament show us, not only the "time" of the fulfillment of the prophecies concerning the sufferings of Christ, but also the *"manner"* of their fulfillment. This is very important and useful; and the main thing to be noted in this connection is that the prophecies concerning the second coming of Christ will be fulfilled, as those relating to His first coming have been fulfilled, *literally*. His coming into the world was a *real* coming. His birth of a virgin was a real birth of a real virgin. His predicted birthplace, Bethlehem, was the real town of that name in Judea. The body of flesh which God "prepared" for Him was a real human body. All His experiences in that body were real human experiences, according to the common lot of men, save only that He was "without sin"—"He did no sin"—He "knew no sin." Likewise, all His predicted sufferings were literally fulfilled with the utmost exactness. He rode into Jerusalem upon a real ass' colt; He was literally betrayed by one of His own familiars; He was taken to a real prison and judgment seat; He was beaten with real stripes, and was nailed to a real "tree," being "lifted up" as Moses lifted up the serpent in the wilderness. He really died, and was really buried in a rich man's sepulchre, and He arose bodily the third day.

All these facts prove beyond question that the many predictions concerning "the glory that should follow" will be fulfilled (in their "time") in the same real, literal, and exact "manner." Let us lay firm hold of this principle of interpretation, and make use of it in our studies.

We take up now the interesting question of the "time" when the predictions concerning the glorious Kingdom of God will be fulfilled, and inquire what the Bible has to tell us about that. We purpose to avoid all doubtful speculation, desiring to go no farther, at present, than we can see our way clearly, according to the "more sure word of prophecy," which is given to us "as a light that shineth in a dark place" (2 Pet. 1:19).

After the resurrection of the Lord Jesus, and just before His ascension into heaven, His disciples asked Him about the "time" of the Kingdom. Being Israelites they were naturally interested to know when the Kingdom would be restored to down-trodden and oppressed Israel. And now that the *sufferings* of Christ were all finished, they were, not unnaturally, eager for "the glories that should follow." So they asked Him, "Lord, wilt Thou at *this time* restore again the Kingdom to *Israel?*" (Acts 1:6).

His reply did not give the information they sought, but directed their attention to *the work which was to be done* before the coming of the promised Kingdom. "And He said unto them, It is not for you to know the times or the seasons, which the Father hath put in His own power. But ye shall receive power, after that the Holy Ghost is come upon you; and ye shall be witnesses unto Me, both in Jerusalem, and in all Judea, and in Samaria, and unto the uttermost part of the earth."

These words of the Lord are not meant to prohibit inquiries concerning the "time" of the Kingdom,—especially on the part of those who are living in the last days of the age. On the contrary, we have every encouragement from the Scriptures to be not ignorant, but "knowing the time," and to realize that the "night is far spent, and *the day* (of the promised Kingdom) is at hand" (Rom. 13:11, 12).

But the disciples chiefly needed, at that time, to learn what God's work was to be *during this age,* which was just then beginning. Notwithstanding what Christ had taught them, when He explained to them the parable of the wheat and tares, and when He answered their questions in Matthew 24, they did not grasp the fact that there was to be a great work of God accomplished between the *sufferings* of Christ and the *glory* that should follow. They had yet to learn what a far-reaching work must needs be done on earth before Christ could "come in His *glory,* and all the holy angels with Him" and could "sit upon the throne of His *glory*" (Matt. 25:31).

So the Lord's reply to the question of the disciples, in Acts 1:6, placed before them the work which they were to do—that is, witnessing to Him in all the world; and it told them of the coming of the Holy Spirit, Who was to empower them for the accomplishment of that work.

This brings us to a very important point; and it is needful that we should clearly understand it before pursuing our inquiry further. It is, however, a point that is very easily understood; and, moreover, it is deeply interesting. We therefore ask close attention to it.

In the light of the New Testament it is clearly seen that the work of Redemption, undertaken by the Son of God, for the glory of God and for the deliverance of sinful men, is divided into *three* eras, or periods of time. Those three eras or periods of time are marked off and distinguished from one another in the clearest way. To know this fact, and to use it, is of the greatest benefit in the study of God's Word; whereas, without it, there must needs be confusion and misunderstanding in regard to the whole subject of *God's purpose* and *His way* of carrying it out. Therefore, we urge our readers to grasp clearly the *three eras* of the work of the Lord Jesus Christ as "the Son of man."

The *first* era comprises "the days of His flesh," covering the thirty-three and a half years of His days on earth, when He humbled Himself, taking "the form of a bond-slave" and was "found in fashion as a man" (Phil. 2:6–8). In other words, the first era or part of our Lord's history as *man*, is the time of "the sufferings of Christ," extending from His birth at Bethlehem to His death at Calvary. That period is *now long past.*

The *second* era is "this present age," during which the Lord Jesus Christ is in heaven, which age is called by many names in the New Testament, as for instance "the acceptable year of the Lord," "the day of salvation," "this present evil age," etc. To this we will return for further consideration.

The *third* era is the coming time of the Lord's return to the earth in power and great "glory," as promised in many Scriptures. That coming time of "the glory" of Christ is the subject into which our present inquiry leads. It is variously called "the day of Christ," the "day of the Lord," "the day of judgment," "the day of vengeance of our God," or sometimes simply "the day" or "that day." The third era of the Lord's history as Son of man will follow immediately upon "the end of this age" now in progress (Matt. 13:40–43, etc.).

And now, inasmuch as the first era is long past, and the second era has already lasted for nearly nineteen hundred years; and since many things have happened, and are happening daily, which make it certain that "the coming of the Lord draweth nigh," it is most appropriate, and also of *the utmost importance* to the people of God that they should have "understanding of the times." Moreover, it is a comparatively easy matter, in our days, to gain a clear understanding of what it most behoves us to know concerning the yet future, but fast approaching, coming and Kingdom of the Son of man.

As a guide to the matter we are now considering,—

the three eras of the work of Christ,—we have taken the words of Hebrews 13:8 for our chapter heading: "Jesus Christ the Same, yesterday, to-day and forever" (or, to the ages).

"Yesterday" is the time of His sufferings on earth "in the days of His flesh."

"To-day" is the age now drawing to a close, during which Christ is in heaven, on His Father's throne, and the Holy Spirit is on earth, speaking to the hearts of men in the Gospel, and saying, *"To-day,* if ye will hear His voice, harden not your hearts" (Heb. 3:7, 8), and during which the people of God are admonished to exhort (or encourage) one another every day, so long as it is called "To-day" (Heb. 3:13).

"Forever" is the age that is to follow immediately upon the present age. It is "the day," which we now can "see approaching," and in which all the prophecies of the *glory* of Christ will be fulfilled.

In all these three eras,—past, present, and future,—He is ever "the Same." As He was "Yesterday," in the days of His humiliation and suffering, so He is "To-day," though crowned with glory and honor in heaven, and so will He be "Forever."

Going back now to Acts 1, we find that immediately after the Lord was taken up from His disciples and a cloud received Him out of their sight, and while they still were gazing up toward heaven, two men stood by them in white apparel, and said: "Ye men of Galilee, why stand ye gazing up into heaven? This *same Jesus,* which is taken up from you into heaven, shall *so* come in *like manner* as ye have seen Him go into heaven" (Acts 1:9–11).

Therefore, notwithstanding the age-long work which lay before them, and notwithstanding that the restoration of Israel was yet a long way in the future, the attention of the disciples was directed *at once,* and in the most definite manner, to the coming again of the Lord Jesus Christ from heaven. For *that* they were to be looking at all times. As He Himself had taught them, they were to watch always, because they knew not what hour their Lord should come (Matt. 24:42, etc.).

Moreover, the promise given to the disciples by the two heavenly messengers tells us that the Coming One is the *"same Jesus"*; and also that the *"manner"* of His coming will be *like that of His going,*—real, bodily, and visible. Thus the fact of His coming again was announced to His disciples immediately upon His departure; and it was declared in the most emphatic way that precisely "as" He went—personally, literally, in bodily presence, seen and known by His disciples—"so" He will return. The statement is too clear to admit of any misunderstanding as to the "manner" of the Lord's coming again.

The three eras of the Lord's history as Son of man can be seen in many Scriptures, and to distinguish those eras adds much to the understanding and enjoyment of the Scriptures themselves. We will therefore refer to several passages, and after examining these, the reader will be able to distinguish for himself the same eras in other Scriptures.

In Hebrews 2 is found a quotation from the Eighth Psalm, in which Psalm the expression "Son of man" occurs for the first time. It is an important Psalm, foretelling the coming time of blessing for creation, when God shall put all things under the feet of "the Son of man." In that Psalm we read: "For Thou hast made Him a little lower than the angels, and hast crowned Him with glory and honor. Thou madest Him to have dominion over the works of Thy hands: Thou hast put all things under His feet" (verses 5, 6).

In Hebrews 2 it is explained that this "Son of man" is the Lord Jesus Christ; and it is further explained that the several things here foretold of Him belong to *the three different periods of time* which we have been considering. For, after quoting the Psalm, the inspired writer of Hebrews says, "But now (at the present time) we see *not yet* all things put under Him": thus plainly declaring that the era of the dominion of the Son of man is *yet in the future.* Then he adds, "But we see Jesus, Who *was* made (in a time already past) a little lower than the angels for the *suffering of death,* crowned with glory and honor." So we learn by this Scripture that the Lord *was made* ("yesterday") a little lower than the angels for the fulfillment of the foretold *sufferings* of Christ; that He is at this present time ("today") crowned with glory and honor in heaven; and that, in a future day, He will have dominion over all the works of God's Hands.

Referring again to Philippians 2, we read that He Who was in the *form of God* "made Himself of no reputation, and took upon Him *the form of a servant,* and *was made* in the likeness of men; and being found in fashion as a man He humbled Himself, and became obedient unto death, the death of the Cross" (verses 6–8). This is easily recognized as a summing-up or epitome of the Lord's life on earth, from His coming into the world in the form of His own creature, to His voluntary death on the cross at the hands of His creatures. Then we read: "Wherefore, God also hath highly exalted Him, and given Him a Name which is above every name." This plainly refers to His present exaltation, in His glorified manhood, at the right hand of God, His Name being now honored above every name.

The next verse brings into view the coming age of His manifested glory, when all things will be subject to Him, and the whole universe will confess Him as Lord: "That at the Name of Jesus every knee should bow, of things in heaven, and things on earth, and things under the earth, and that every tongue should confess that Jesus Christ is Lord, to the glory of God the Father" (Phil. 2:9, 10).

Of these three eras of our Lord's life as man, the first, which embraced the days of His sufferings, and which is called "yesterday," is now long past; and the second, embracing the time when He sits on His Father's throne in heaven, that is "to-day," is far spent. Hence the third era is close at hand, and any day may bring the fulfillment of His promise: "After *this* I will return."

III

MY CHURCH

IT is needful at this point that we should learn from the Scriptures just what work God has purposed to accomplish in this long age, which He has interposed between "the sufferings of Christ and the glory that should (and will) follow." For the beginning of the next age necessarily awaits the completion of the work which, in God's great plan (formed before the creation of the world), has been assigned to the age in which we are now living. But, apart from that, God's present work is of surpassing interest, and it is the privilege of those who are of the faith of Jesus Christ to look into it and observe its progress.

As a suitable starting point for the study of this part of our subject, we turn to Matthew 16, verses 13 to 28. In those verses we shall find again the three eras of our Lord's history, and also shall find, in His own words, a brief statement of what belongs to each of these three periods. The passage is one of the most important in the Bible, and no amount of study can exhaust its contents:

"When Jesus came into the coasts of Cæsarea Philippi, He asked His disciples, saying, Whom do men say that I, the Son of man, am? And

> they said, Some say that Thou art John the Baptist; some Elias; and others Jeremias, or one of the prophets."

The answer reveals the dense spiritual darkness of the nation, particularly of the respectable and educated part thereof, including the scribes and doctors of the law. As Paul said, at a later day, "they that dwell at Jerusalem, and their rulers, because *they knew Him not,* nor yet the voices of the prophets which are read every Sabbath day, they have fulfilled them in condemning Him" (Acts 13:27). And as recorded by John, "He was in the world, and the world was made by Him, and the world *knew Him not*" (John 1:10).

After hearing the answer of the disciples, He further asked, "But whom say *ye* that I am?" And Simon Peter answered and said,

> "Thou art the Christ the Son of the living God. And Jesus answered and said unto him, Blessed art thou, Simon Bar-jona: for flesh and blood hath not revealed it unto thee, but My Father which is in heaven. And I say unto thee, that thou art Peter; and upon this rock I will build My Church; and the gates of hell shall not prevail against it. And I will give unto thee the keys of the Kingdom of heaven: and whatsoever thou shalt bind on earth shall be bound in heaven; and whatsoever thou shalt loose on earth shall be loosed in heaven."

In order to grasp the significance of this event, and of these words of the Lord, it is necessary to refer to the Second Psalm. In the light of that great prophetic Psalm we can understand, in some measure at least, the meaning of Peter's reply to the Lord's question, and the meaning of His comment thereon.

The Second Psalm is the only Old Testament Scripture, except Proverbs 30:4, that refers to the "Son" of God. In that Psalm One is mentioned to Whom God addresses those remarkable words: "Thou art My Son, this day have I begotten Thee." That the One thus addressed is not merely a man or other created being appears clearly by the words: "Blessed are all they that put their trust in Him." That the "Son" here referred to could not be "*man*," or any creature, is clear, because it is written, "Thus saith the Lord, *Cursed* be the man that trusteth in man" (Jer. 17:5).

Furthermore, in the Second Psalm, kings and rulers of the earth are counselled to submit themselves to the Son, else they will be in danger of His wrath; and it is declared that, by God's decree, when the Son shall ask of Him, He shall give Him *the nations* of the world for His inheritance, and the *uttermost parts* of the earth for His possession. This portion of the prophecy we have no difficulty in placing in the approaching age of Christ's glory.

Further, the Psalm speaks of a commotion among the people and of a stand taken by the kings and rulers of the earth against the Lord, and against His Anointed—that is to say, His Messiah or Christ. (The three words—Anointed, Messiah, and Christ—have exactly the same meaning.) Thus we have also, in this Psalm, a direct mention of the "Christ" of God by name; and the words used in this connection (verses 1, 2) indicate His rejection by the rulers of this world. This part of the prophecy (verses 1, 2) is located for us by the words of the disciples recorded in Acts 4:24–28, where, after quoting those verses, they said: "For of a truth, against Thy holy child Jesus, Whom Thou hast *anointed,* both Herod, and Pontius Pilate, with the Gentiles, and the people of Israel, were gathered together, for to do whatsoever Thy hand and Thy counsel determined before to be done." That part, therefore, of the prophecy has been fulfilled. It clearly belongs to the period of the Lord's days on earth ("yesterday").

Again the Psalm declares that the rejection of Christ, the Son of God, by the rulers of earth will not be allowed to defeat God's purpose. For we read, "He that sitteth in the heavens shall laugh; the Lord shall have them in derision. Then shall He speak unto them in His wrath, and vex them in His sore displeasure. *Yet have I set My King* upon my holy hill of Zion." This part of the prophecy clearly belongs to the future age of Christ's earthly glory.

All believing Israelites, knowing of the purposes of God declared in this prophecy, were always eagerly looking for the One by Whom those purposes were to be accomplished, God's King, the Messiah, the Son of the living God.

When, therefore, Peter gave utterance to the confession recorded in Matthew 16:16, it was virtually to say, "THOU art the One foretold in the Second Psalm. Thou art the Christ, the Son of the living God." Thus Peter gave utterance to the mighty

Truth, the Rock Foundation, upon which saving faith is based. That knowledge comes not by flesh and blood, but by revelation of the Father. For we have the Lord's own words that "No man knoweth the Son but the Father" (Matt. 11:27). To the world He is the carpenter's son, the man of Galilee, or at most John the Baptist, or Elijah, or one of the prophets. But to faith He is the Christ, the Son of the living God.

We do not attempt, in this volume, to point out the various bearings of the incident now before us; but purpose to confine ourselves to the consideration of its relation to the subject of the first and second comings of Christ, and to the interval or "age" that lies between. That intervening age is not seen in the Second Psalm, which is in harmony with all Old Testament prophecies in overlooking it. But now, in making Himself known as the Person who is the subject of that prophecy, the Lord proceeds at once to separate the era of His *sufferings* from that of His *glory* (a separation which does not appear in the Psalm itself) and also to speak distinctly of *what was to intervene.* In His words to Peter, which we have quoted, He mentions two subjects: (1) "MY CHURCH"; and (2) "THE KINGDOM OF HEAVEN." Those subjects are distinct from each other, though related; and it is important both to distinguish clearly between them, and also to understand how they are related. The Lord spoke of His Church as a thing *yet future.* "I *will* build My Church"; and this is the first mention of the Church, whereas the Kingdom of heaven had already been publicly announced, the Kingdom of heaven being the subject that is most prominently connected with His first coming. Both Christ and His disciples, and before them, John the Baptist, had already proclaimed the Kingdom of heaven as "at hand."

Of the Church, Christ speaks as of a thing peculiarly *His own*—"*My* Church." To the same effect in Acts 20:28, we read of "the Church *of God*, which He hath purchased with His own blood." And in Ephesians 5:25–27 this peculiar personal relation is strongly stated in the words, "Husbands, love your wives, even as Christ also loved the Church and *gave Himself for it;* that *He* might sanctify and cleanse it with the washing of water by the Word, that *He* might present it *to Himself* a glorious Church (lit., a Church of *glory*) not having spot, or wrinkle, or any such thing, but that it might be holy and without blemish."

Moreover, Christ keeps the building of the Church in His own hands, saying: "*I* will build My Church." The Church is thus declared to be His, not only as purchased with His own blood, and because He is its Head and Lord, but also because He is its Builder. The same truth of Christ's exclusive proprietorship of the Church is expressed in the passage from Ephesians, "that *He* might present it to Himself."

In the passage in Matthew 16, the Lord did not assign to Peter any office or duty in connection with His *Church*, but He did promise to that apostle an important post in connection with the *Kingdom of heaven* which was about to be inaugurated, saying, "I will give unto thee the keys of the Kingdom of heaven." The fulfillment of this promise is seen in the action of Peter on the day of Pentecost when he preached Jesus risen from the dead as "both Lord and Christ," and when, as the result of his testimony and exhortation, "there were added unto them about three thousand souls." Thus was the door of the Kingdom of heaven opened by Peter to the Jews. And, again, at the house of Cornelius, Peter was the one specially selected and prepared by a vision and by verbal instructions from the Lord to throw open the door of the Kingdom to a company of Gentiles. As Peter himself said, when speaking to the Church at Jerusalem: "Men and brethren, ye know how that a good while ago God made choice among us that the Gentiles, *by my mouth,* should hear *the word of the Gospel* and believe" (Acts 15:7). Thus it is clearly seen that the Gospel is the key whereby Peter opened the door of the Kingdom of heaven to both Jews and Gentiles. It is further seen that the Kingdom of heaven, which the Lord had announced as "at hand," began formally at Pentecost when 3,000 Jews were born of the Word and Spirit of God.

The door of the Kingdom of heaven, which was duly opened by the Apostle Peter at the appointed time, still is wide open, and God's invitation to enter into it, which the Gospel gives to all the world, has not yet been recalled. For God wishes "all men to be saved, and to come unto the knowledge of the truth" (1 Tim. 2:4). Hence His servants still are commanded to say to all men everywhere, "Come, for all things are ready." God has waited long, and still waits, in order that every opportunity may be given to perishing sinners to escape the judgment and wrath to come, and to enter into all the blessings and benefits of that wonderful Kingdom. But it should be observed that, while the Lord gave to Peter the keys of the Kingdom of heaven, He keeps in His own hands "the key of David." No one has been delegated to open the Kingdom of the glory of the Son of man. It is for Him to decide who are to be "accounted worthy" to enter that Kingdom and to "stand before the Son of man" (Matt. 25:31–34; Luke 21:36; 2 Thess. 1:5, 11).

It should be specially noted that, when the Lord Jesus was recognized and acknowledged by His disciples as the Christ of Old Testament prophecy, He immediately announced the purpose of His mission, speaking of His Church—a new subject—and also of the Kingdom of heaven. Moreover, from *that time forth* He began to show to His disciples that He *must* go to Jerusalem, and suffer many things of the elders and chief priests and scribes, and be killed, and be raised again the third day. It is evident from the connection in which this revelation was made, and is also evident from other Scriptures, that the reason why Christ "must" suffer those things was because only in that way could the Church be built and the Kingdom of heaven be introduced. And since "Christ *must needs* have suffered and risen again from the dead" (Acts 17:3), or in other words, since the Christ of God must needs be One Who died and rose again according to the Scriptures, we see clearly the reason for the Lord's charging His disciples, previously to His death and resurrection, that they should, as yet, tell no man that He, Jesus, was the Christ (Matt. 16:20). Christ could not be preached, according to the plan and purpose of God, *until* He had died on the tree and had risen from the dead.

It will be readily seen that the things which are said of the Church could not be said of the Kingdom of heaven. Christ did not say: "I will build My Kingdom." Nor did Paul say: "Christ loved the Kingdom and gave Himself for it." Hence it is quite clear that the Church of Christ and the Kingdom of heaven are not one and the same thing, but are to be distinguished.

On the other hand, it is equally clear that the Church and the Kingdom of heaven are closely related. We merely note these facts here, purposing later on to show in what way the two great subjects which the Lord mentioned in His response to Peter's confession are related, and also wherein they differ.

The Lord's words, "I will build My Church," tell us that the Church is a building, and that the Builder thereof is *the Lord Himself*. Both facts are of the highest importance.

To David's son, it had been given by promise both to occupy the throne of God's *Kingdom* and also *to build the house of God;* and "the House of God is the Church of the living God, the pillar and ground of the truth" (1 Tim. 3:15).

The building of the Church of Christ is, therefore, an important part of the work of the present age; and when we learn all that the Scripture has to tell us of the nature and the grandeur of that "holy temple" that is being built of "living stones" for "an habitation of God through the Spirit" (Eph. 2:20–22; 1 Pet. 2:4–6), we shall not wonder at the length of time which God has assigned to its completion.

If the temple that Solomon was to build was to be "exceeding magnifical"; if it required vast and costly preparations on the part of David, and long and careful work by the most skilled workmen to raise it up—only to be entirely destroyed after a comparatively brief time,—who can conceive, or find words to describe, that *Church of glory,* which David's greater Son (for "a greater than Solomon is here") is now building, at His own cost, for God's eternal habitation, and through which even "*now,* unto the principalities and powers in heavenly places, the manifold wisdom of God" is made known? (Eph. 3:10).

We have stated that in Matthew 16 the three eras of the Lord's history as Son of man are to be found: we will now point them out.

Following the verses we have already quoted, we read: "Then charged He His disciples that they should tell no man that He was Jesus the Christ" (more literally, "that He, Jesus, was the Christ"). Since He had not come to reign on earth, but to suffer and die,—not to ascend the throne of David, but to be lifted up on a cross—He forbade that He should be preached as "the Christ" until He had accomplished the appointed "sufferings of Christ," and offered the appointed sacrifice as "the Lamb of God." "The Christ," who was to be preached as the object of saving faith, must be Christ crucified and raised from the dead. He must be One Who had already "suffered" the things foretold of Him. So we note with deepest interest the next words: "From that time forth began Jesus to show unto His disciples, how that He *must* go unto Jerusalem, and *suffer* many things of the elders and chief priests and scribes, and be killed, and rise again the third day." It should be specially noted that the Lord Jesus so far from announcing Himself to the Jews as the Christ of God, actually forbade those disciples who recognized Him to proclaim Him as such.

And now that the Lord was acknowledged as "the Christ," He began at once to teach the disciples concerning the appointed "*sufferings* of Christ." It was a new subject to them, and one they were most unwilling to receive. As Israelites they longed for the coming of the promised and long expected King, Who should deliver their nation from the yoke of the Roman oppressor. And now the King had indeed come. Then surely the hope of Israel was about to be realized. So Peter "began to rebuke Him, saying, Be it far from Thee, Lord: this shall not be unto Thee." But in thus setting himself against the purpose of God, upon which the work of Redemption, and also the building of the Church and the introducing of the Kingdom of heaven depended, Peter was acting as the mouthpiece of Satan. Consequently, he thereby brought upon himself the severe rebuke: "Get thee behind Me, Satan; for thou savorest not the things that be of God, but those that be of men."

The sufferings and death of Christ were "the things that be of God," for on them the salvation of God depended; whereas the idea of mere political deliverance from the Roman yoke would readily appeal to men.

Thus the Lord definitely placed His own betrayal, sufferings, death and resurrection in that day of His first coming. It was the great purpose for which He came, and without which His incarnation would have been in vain. So here we find the first of the three eras defined in the preceding chapter.

The words, "I will build My Church, and the gates of hell" (the place of the dead) "shall not prevail against it," declare the work of this long age, during which Christ is on the right hand of God in heaven, and the Holy Spirit is in the world, giving power to the preaching of the Gospel, quickening those who believe, baptizing them into the body of Christ, the Church, and dwelling in them. These things belong to the second era—"to-day."

The third era is clearly set forth in the words of verse 27: "For the Son of man *shall come in the glory of the Father* with His angels, and then shall He reward every man according to his works."

Christ Himself is the Rock of Ages upon which His Church is built. No other foundation would support God's "spiritual house." The Lord Himself showed this when, in speaking to the Pharisees, He said: "Did ye never read in the scriptures, The stone which the builders rejected, the same is become the head of the corner: this is the Lord's doing and it is marvellous in our eyes?" (Matt. 21:42).

To the same effect the Apostle Paul said: "Other Foundation can no man lay than that is laid, which is Jesus Christ" (1 Cor. 3:11).

But Peter himself is the chief witness to the truth here presented. Speaking to the Jewish rulers, the high priest and the authorities of the temple, he testified of the power that is in the Name of Jesus of Nazareth, and said: "This is the Stone which was set at nought of you builders, which is become the head of the corner" (Acts 4:11).

And in his first Epistle, speaking to and of those who have been born again of the incorruptible seed of the Word of God, which "by the Gospel" had been preached to them, the Apostle said: "As newborn babes, desire the sincere milk of the Word, that ye may grow thereby: if so be ye have tasted that the Lord is gracious. To Whom coming, as unto a *living Stone,* disallowed indeed of men, but chosen of God and precious, ye also, as living stones, are *built up* a spiritual house, an holy priesthood, to offer up spiritual sacrifices, acceptable to God by Jesus Christ. Wherefore also it is contained in the Scripture, Behold I lay in Zion a *chief corner stone,* elect, precious: and he that believeth *on Him* shall not be confounded" (1 Pet. 2:2–6).

All who believe on the Lord Jesus Christ are "living stones" and are being built up together to form that "spiritual house." And though the work be long, yet it will have an end, even as the building of Solomon's temple was at last finished. And then the Builder will return and will present it to Himself "a Church of glory"; according to the faithful promise: "After this I will return, and will build again the tabernacle of David, which is fallen down" (Acts 15:16). •In the present age He is building His Church, and that must needs be completed and ready to be presented to Himself ere His promised return. But when He shall have finished building His Church, then He will return and *build again* the tabernacle of David. Shall not we then, who "belong to Christ," seek earnestly to know our place as individuals in "the Church, which is His body," and give the utmost diligence to the doing of our part in the work thereof?

"In Him it is ordained to raise
A temple to Jehovah's praise,
Composed of all the saints who own
No Saviour but the 'Living Stone.'

"View the vast building, see it rise!
The work, how great! the plan, how wise!
O wondrous fabric, power unknown
That rears it on the 'Living Stone.'"

IV

THE KINGDOM OF HEAVEN

WE come now to a great subject that has been much misunderstood, and consequently much neglected.

We have seen how the Lord Jesus, at the time when His disciples recognized Him as "the Christ, the Son of the living God," immediately mentioned two objects of His coming into the world: (1) *the Church,* and (2) *the Kingdom;* and how He made an important announcement in regard to each. By His devotion to those two objects the Lord showed Himself to be the true Son of David: for God promised to David a Son of Whom *two things* were foretold,—first, that He should "build" *the house of God,* and second, that God would establish *His throne* forever. We shall not attempt to refer to the many prophecies in which these two things concerning David's promised Son were foretold. For our purpose it will suffice to refer to 1 Chronicles 17, where God, through Nathan the prophet, made promise to David, saying, "I will raise up of thy seed after thee, which shall be of thy sons, and I will establish *His Kingdom.* He shall *build Me a house,* and I will establish *His throne* forever" (verses 11, 12).

In the words, "I will build My Church," Christ undertakes the accomplishment of the work of building God a house; for "the house of God is the Church of the living God" (1 Tim. 3:15; Eph. 2:20–22, etc.).

David's son, Solomon, is a type of Jesus Christ; for Solomon's reign was one of peace, of wonderful prosperity, and of unequalled glory; and, moreover, Solomon was chosen of God to build the temple. Solomon was specially endowed with *wisdom* beyond all other men. And Solomon said: "Through *wisdom* is a house builded." And again: "*Wisdom* hath builded her house, she hath hewn out her seven pillars" (Prov. 24:3; 9:1, 2). To Solomon, therefore, God gave *power* and *wisdom* for the administration of the *Kingdom,* and for the building of the house of God.

But in Christ we see "a greater than Solomon." For Christ is "the Power of God and the Wisdom of God" (1 Cor. 1:24). And the house of God, which He is building, far surpasses the temple of Solomon, which was but a "shadow" of God's "spiritual house," through which is made known, to the principalities and powers in heavenly places, "the manifold WISDOM of God" (Eph. 3:10).

We have seen that the building of the Church, "for an habitation of God," is one feature of the great work of the present age. But what becomes of the Kingdom of heaven? This is a subject to which it were well for us to give our best attention.

Turning back to Matthew 13, we find the Lord speaking to His disciples of "the mysteries of the Kingdom of heaven," telling them that it was *given to them* to know those mysteries, but that to the mass of unbelieving Jews it was not given (verse 11). In verse 35, the Lord states that the "mysteries" referred to were "things which have been *kept secret* from the foundation of the world." But those things, formerly "kept secret," are now "made known." They are not "mysteries" in the ordinary sense of that word, nor are they any longer among the "secret things" which "belong to the Lord"; for He Himself has now revealed them. "The secret things belong unto the Lord our God; but those things which are *revealed* belong unto us and to our children forever" (Deut. 29:29).[1]

The parables recorded in Matthew 13 were spoken by the Lord for the express purpose of revealing to His disciples (and to none other) certain important facts concerning the Kingdom of heaven which, though they were always in the purpose of God "from the foundation of the world," had been kept secret up to that time, not having been revealed to the prophets of old. To those prophets had been given a very full and detailed revelation concerning the Kingdom as it is to be in the next age, and which the Lord Jesus calls—not the "Kingdom of heaven" but—"the Kingdom of the Son of man." One of the clearest Old Testament prophecies concerning *that* Kingdom is found in the book of Daniel, who describes, in chapter 7, a vision in which he saw

[1] I am indebted to a tract entitled "The Kingdom of Heaven and the Kingdom of the Son of Man," by John James, for calling attention to Scriptural proof that the Kingdom of heaven belongs in this present age and the Kingdom of the Son of Man in the succeeding age. This is a fact which the evidence of Scripture establishes conclusively, and is, moreover, a fact of great importance.

various kingdoms that were to arise. In the vision those kingdoms appeared in the form of wild beasts. And he saw further:

> "And behold, one like the *Son of man* came with the clouds of heaven and came to the Ancient of Days, and they brought Him near before Him. And there was given Him dominion and glory and a kingdom, that all people, nations, and languages should serve Him; His dominion is an everlasting dominion which shall not pass away, and His Kingdom that which shall not be destroyed" (Dan. 7:13, 14).

We call special attention to the fact that the Kingdom seen in Daniel's vision is that of "the Son of man." It is important to note this, because it throws light upon certain passages in which the Lord spoke of the Kingdom of "the Son of man," showing that, in those passages, He was referring expressly to the Kingdom *as it will be in the age to come,* when "all people, nations and languages shall serve Him." (See Matt. 13:41; 16:27, 28; 19:28; 25:31; 26:64.) The Old Testament prophecies tell many things concerning that glorious Kingdom of the Son of man, which will extend over all the earth, bringing peace, happiness and unspeakable blessings to all peoples. But those Old Testament prophecies are absolutely silent as regards the "Kingdom of heaven," that is to say, the Kingdom in the peculiar form it was to take (and has taken) throughout this present age. All things concerning the Kingdom of heaven were "mysteries" or secret things, in Old Testament times.

But when John the Baptist, the Lord's forerunner, appeared, as foretold in Isaiah 40, and Malachi 4, he proclaimed "the Kingdom of heaven" as being "at hand," and preached the baptism of repentance to Israel. It is important to note, in this connection, that John did not proclaim national deliverance for Israel, nor did he proclaim the promised Deliverer; and so far as the record shows, he did not once mention "Christ." The record of John's proclamation, as given in Matthew, is in these words:

> "I indeed baptize you with water unto repentance; but He that cometh after me is mightier than I, Whose shoes I am not able to bear; He shall *baptize you with the Holy Ghost and with fire;* whose fan is in His hand, and He will throughly purge His floor, and gather His wheat into the garner; but He will burn up the chaff with unquenchable fire" (Matt. 3:11, 12).

In considering this announcement of John (which was made before the Lord Jesus appeared on the scene) careful attention should be given to the terms in which the Coming One was described, and to the statement of what He was to do. For it is necessary at this point to establish the important fact that the Kingdom of heaven belongs *in this present age,* and that it has not been displaced or "postponed" (as we are sometimes told) while in the meantime the Church is being built. For it is quite commonly taught, and by some who are very gifted as expositors of Scripture, that the proclamation of the Kingdom of heaven by John and by the Lord Himself and His disciples, was an offer of national deliverance to Israel and of the setting up of an earthly kingdom, as foretold in the Old Testament prophecies; that the offer, however, was *conditional,* and was intended to be made good *only in case the Jews should accept the Lord Jesus as their King;* that when He offered Himself as their King they rejected Him, in consequence whereof the offer was "withdrawn," and that Christ thereupon announced, as an alternative plan, that He would build His Church, pending which the Kingdom of heaven is said to be "postponed," or to be "in abeyance."

The foregoing theory is based upon the assumption that, when God announced through John the Baptist that the Kingdom of heaven was at hand, He was offering to Israel deliverance from the yoke of Rome, and the restoration of the throne of David. It is based, also, upon the further assumption that Christ's offer of Himself to the Jews as their King was a *conditional offer,* depending wholly upon their acceptance of it. And the theory is based upon the still further assumption that the building of the Church was an *alternative* undertaking, to which the Lord turned after His offer of the Kingdom to Israel had been "rejected." Those assumptions are one and all erroneous, as we propose to show by the clearest testimony from the Scriptures. The facts in this regard are:

(1) That the proclamation of the "Kingdom of heaven" was *not* the offer of *earthly dominion to Israel.* That, indeed, has been promised in the Scriptures, and will be fulfilled in its due season, namely, at the Lord's second coming. But the

proclamation of the "Kingdom of heaven" made at Christ's first coming was just what it purported to be, namely, the unqualified declaration of God's purpose—as determined in His secret counsels "from the foundation of the world"—to introduce into "the world," at this stage of His great plan, a Kingdom of *heavenly* character;

(2) That the proclamation of the Kingdom of heaven was *not conditional at all* on anything that the Jews might or might not do, or upon any contingency whatever, but was an absolutely unconditional announcement of a settled fact, namely, that the Kingdom of heaven was "at hand," or in other words, was about to be introduced;

(3) That the building of the Church is not an *alternative plan,* brought forward after the Kingdom was temporarily abandoned or postponed, but is, and always was, a fixed part of God's purpose for this age, and the accomplishment of which proceeds hand in hand with the spreading of the Kingdom of heaven throughout "the world."

The evidence of Scripture in support of the simple propositions we have advanced above is incontrovertible and overwhelming; whereas the assumptions we are opposing have contrived somehow, and through whatever agency we know not, to gain a rather wide acceptance *without the assistance of a scintilla of Bible evidence in their favor.* And this we expect to make quite clear to our readers. Moreover, it should be remembered that there is every likelihood that the things which the Lord Jesus Christ did and suffered on earth were the very things that were purposed of God, and that God's plan, in sending forth His Son, could not possibly be controlled, shaped, or influenced by the actions of men. It is a strange thought, indeed, that the sublime and immutable purpose of Him Who worketh all things after the counsel of His own will, could depend in any wise upon what His creatures might or might not do. There is every presumption in favor of the view that, when God announced the Kingdom of heaven to be at hand, it *was* at hand. The contrary view should not be adopted except upon the most convincing testimony; and the testimony is all the other way.

Returning now to the terms of John's proclamation, as found in the first Gospel, we note that the Lord was not announced as a *King* coming to take the throne, or as a political Deliverer, and was not even announced as the Christ. John described Him as "He that cometh after me," saying of Him that "He is mightier than I, Whose shoes I am not worthy to bear." There is no hint here of political independence for the Jews, nor is there such a hint in any other announcement, whether by John, or by the Lord Himself, or by His disciples, but quite the contrary. There can be no doubt that, if Christ *had offered Himself* to the Jews as a *political leader* and sought to promote an insurrection against the Romans, the people would have accepted Him with enthusiasm, and would have flocked to His support. The instructive incidents of Theudas and of Judas of Galilee (Acts 5:36, 37) show what would have happened in such a case.

Moreover, the fact is, and it is a very significant fact indeed, that Barabbas, whom Pilate released to the Jews, at their request, was a man who had been the leader of an insurrection (Mark 15:7). Thus, whereas the Lord was falsely accused of "forbidding to give tribute to Cæsar, saying that He Himself is Christ a King" (Luke 23:2), the truth was just the reverse, for Christ commanded that His disciples should render to Cæsar the things that were Cæsar's (Luke 20:25); while on the other hand, Barabbas, a *notable* prisoner, who had led an insurrection against the authority of Rome, was pardoned at the request of the Jews.

Furthermore, in John's announcement of what the One that was to come after him would do, we have clear and ample evidence (even without going any further) that Christ came with no thought or suggestion of any earthly kingdom, but to do and suffer exactly what subsequently happened. "He shall baptize you," said John, "with the Holy Ghost and with fire." Here we have *the two events which mark, respectively, the beginning and the ending of the Kingdom of heaven.* That Kingdom began when the disciples were baptized with the Holy Ghost at Pentecost. So the very first thing announced by John the Baptist, when he proclaimed the Kingdom of heaven as "at hand," was something that could not take place until after Christ should have died and risen and ascended into heaven. (See John 7:39 and Acts 1:5.) Moreover, from the parable of the Tares of the Field, it is clear (as will be seen later on) that the Kingdom of heaven was inaugurated by *preaching the Gospel of Christ,* and the preaching of that message necessarily awaited the coming of the Holy Ghost from heaven. Thus, it clearly appears that John's announcement looked forward to the day of Pentecost for its fulfillment, and necessarily involved the Lord's death, resurrection and ascension. All of those stupendous events prepared the way for the introduction of the Kingdom of heaven by the preaching of Christ among all nations of the world, "with the Holy Ghost sent down from heaven."

It is clear that the Kingdom of heaven was fully inaugurated by the baptism with the Holy Ghost, announced by John the Baptist, and fulfilled on the day of Pentecost. The period of the Lord's ministry "in the days of His flesh" was preliminary, and belongs, in a sense, to the era of the Kingdom (see Matt. 11:12; 23:13), though it was not fully inaugurated until Pentecost.

The announcement by John of the baptism "with fire" foretells with equal clearness what will happen at the *end* of this age, when the Lord Jesus will be revealed from heaven "in flaming *fire*" (2 Thess. 1:7, 8). From John's words it is transparently clear that the baptism with "fire" refers to the destruction of the wicked at the end of this age, for verse 12 (of Matt. 3) distinctly declares that the Lord will throughly purge His winnowing floor, "and gather *His wheat* into the garner; but He will burn up the chaff with unquenchable *fire.*" Turning to Matthew 13:40–42, where the Lord explains in simple language the parable of the tares, we find that what John had thus announced before the Lord Himself appeared on the scene is precisely what will take place at the end of the Kingdom of heaven. The rapture of the saints brings the Kingdom of heaven to an end; and then comes the Kingdom of the Son of man, with its baptism of fire.

It follows that there was no change at all in God's purpose in sending His Son into the world, no deviation whatever from His plan. The course of events moved straight forward in the line of God's "determinate counsel and foreknowledge" (Acts 3:23). His purpose from the foundation of the world, as proclaimed by John the Baptist, and as revealed by the Lord in His parables, was to bring in an age of "Grace" for the whole world, based upon the sacrificial death of His own Son and His resurrection from the dead, during which age the Church was to be built, and the Kingdom of heaven was to be introduced by the preaching of the Gospel of Christ among all the nations of the world (the "Gentiles").

The account of John's message, as given by Mark and Luke, does not differ materially from the above. That of Luke adds interesting matters, but all that is recorded tends to exclude the idea that an earthly kingdom, or a political change of any kind, was announced, or was contemplated. The record given in John's Gospel makes that idea absolutely untenable. For John, seeing Jesus coming to him, said, "Behold the LAMB OF GOD, which taketh away the sin of the world" (John 1:29). We shall refer again to this Scripture.

The first public act of the Lord Jesus was His

baptism, upon which (though John forbade it) He insisted, saying, "Suffer it to be so now, for thus it becometh us to fulfill all righteousness" (Matt. 3:15). Thus the Lord, at the very commencement of His ministry, enacted the symbol of His own burial and resurrection, declaring thereby the object for which He had come into the world. That object was as different as possible from the setting up of an earthly kingdom, and the occupying of an earthly throne.

In this connection, attention should be given to the fact that baptism stands conspicuously at the threshold of the Kingdom of heaven. It has been appointed by God for those entering His Kingdom; but, in perfect keeping with the character of that Kingdom, it is not compulsory. And surely no compulsion should be needed. Baptism should be regarded, as it was by the first disciples, as a happy privilege accorded to those whose sins are forgiven through the death and resurrection of the Lord Jesus Christ. In the early days the question was—not what is the need of baptism, or how is it to be administered, but—"What doth *hinder me* to be baptized?" and "Can any man *forbid* water?" (Acts 8:36; 10:47). For it has been truly said that "baptism effects nothing, but it *expresses much.*" What is just now to the point is that it expresses, on the part of the forgiven sinner, the great truth that he has died with Christ, and is raised with Him, to serve God as one who is "alive from the dead." This is according to Romans 6:1–17, a passage that is full of Kingdom-truth.

In the face of these (and many other) conclusive

proofs to the contrary, it is difficult to conceive how any who expound and teach the Scriptures can maintain for a moment that the Lord's first coming had any political purpose in view, or that He came with any other object before Him than that which He Himself declared, namely, "to give His life a ransom for many."

The Scriptures will be searched in vain for any occasion on which the Lord offered Himself to the Jews as their King, or where He ever hinted in the remotest way at national deliverance, or at the possibility of His acceptance of the throne of David, or at anything of that nature. John 6:14, 15 is a Scripture that completely overthrows that idea. There we read that, following the miracle of feeding the five thousand, "Then those men, when they had seen the miracle that Jesus did, said, This is of a truth that Prophet that should come into the world. When Jesus therefore perceived that they would come and take Him by force *to make Him a King,* He departed again into a mountain Himself alone."

This is the only occasion when there was mention of making Him a King, and He, so far from having proposed it, was the One Who suppressed the movement. The Kingdom which He came to establish at that time, and which His forerunner proclaimed, was a very different sort of Kingdom, being altogether *unearthly* in character. It was a Kingdom which required, for its introduction, not that He should overthrow the Roman power and bring Gentile governments to an end, but that He should be betrayed to that very Roman power, and be put to death by crucifixion (a form of death inflicted by the Romans), as was specifically foretold in Psalm 22:16. Christ is, of course, the King of the Jews, and He acknowledged it in response to the question of Pilate (Matt. 27:11). But He never offered Himself to Israel as their King, which is quite another matter. The occasion that came nearest to it was His last entrance into Jerusalem. But that incident itself refutes the theory of an offer of an earthly Kingdom to Israel, for (*a*) it occurred at the *end* of His ministry, long after the supposed rejection by Israel of the earthly Kingdom; and (*b*) it was the fulfillment of Zechariah 9:9, which says: "Behold thy King cometh unto thee; He is *just and having salvation;* lowly and riding upon an ass, and upon a colt the foal of an ass." His predicted coming was, therefore, as the *Saviour,* not to reign, but to die "the Just" for the unjust, that He might bring us to God (cf. 1 Pet. 3:18). At His first coming He was "lowly" and "riding upon an ass." At His second coming, to establish the Kingdom of Old Testament prophecy, He will be very exalted, riding upon "a white horse"—and having upon His head "many crowns" (Rev. 20:11-16).

The Name that was given Him before His birth, and the reason assigned for the bestowal of that Name, utterly preclude the idea that deliverance for the nation of Israel was in contemplation. "He shall save His people from their *sins*" (Matt. 1:21),—that was what His Name pledged Him to accomplish. Those words declare in the plainest way the purpose for which He came into the world. In order to save His people from their sins He Himself must needs bear them in His own body on the tree. There was *no other way;* and it is perhaps the most serious feature of the view we are opposing, that it makes the Cross, and all that eternally depended upon it, a matter that was contingent upon the uncertain actions of men.

There are some expositors of repute who claim to be able to tell us what *would have* happened if Christ's offer to the Jews of an earthly Kingdom (which "offer," however, was never made or contemplated) had been accepted by them. For they tell us that, in such an event, He would at once have ascended the throne of His father David, and fulfilled the Old Testament prophecies of the Kingdom of the Son of man. How and whence those expositors procured this remarkable information does not appear. That events could possibly have taken such a course as to remove the Cross from its central place in God's plan, to eliminate entirely the day of grace and the preaching of Christ crucified and risen from the dead as God's salvation to the ends of the earth, is the wildest sort of speculation that the human mind could possibly indulge in. One of those who hold and propagate that view was asked recently how, in the conjectured event of Christ's ascending the throne of David at His first coming, the work of Redemption would have been accomplished, and he replied that it would have been accomplished in *some other way*. But the Lord Himself knew of no other way; for when His deliverance from His captors was attempted He said: "But *how then shall the Scriptures be fulfilled that* THUS IT MUST BE?" (Matt. 26:54). He saw no "other way" of accomplishing the work of Redemption than the way of the Cross; for "Himself He could not save." That cry in the garden, "Father, *if it* BE *possible,* let this cup pass from Me," scatters to the winds the baseless speculation on which we are commenting. It was NOT *"possible."*

Turning to the Lord's own personal ministry, we find in His words and deeds no hint of any offer of earthly deliverance to Israel; but we find, on the contrary, abundant evidence that nothing of that sort was in contemplation. He went about all Galilee teaching in their synagogues, and preaching the Gospel of the Kingdom, and healing all manner of sickness and all manner of disease among the people. What He taught concerning the Kingdom of heaven is given with all needed fullness and clearness in the "Sermon on the Mount." In that discourse, so far from offering national deliverance and earthly supremacy to His disciples *at that time,* He pictured to them a state of things exactly the reverse. They were to be persecuted, reviled and spoken against for His sake. They were not to resist evil, but when smitten on one cheek to turn the other. They were to love their enemies, to return blessing for cursing, and to pray for those who despitefully used them and persecuted them. Every word He uttered was absolutely inconsistent with the idea that He came for earthly conquest and dominion, and on the other hand was in perfect keeping with the fact that His path to the throne was a path of suffering, which led to the cross and the tomb. Nothing else was before Him at any time in His days on earth. He was born "a Saviour" (Luke 2:11; Matt. 1:27); and when He was an infant of thirty days, Simeon (the Holy Spirit being upon him) said to His mother: "Behold, this child is set for the fall and rising again of many in Israel, and for a sign which shall be *spoken against;* yea, a sword shall pierce through thine own soul also" (Luke 2:25–35).

Matthew 10 is another passage that affords conclusive evidence on the point under consideration. There we have an account of the sending forth of the twelve to "preach, saying, The Kingdom of heaven is at hand." In the words which the Lord spoke when sending forth that announcement we have the clearest evidence that the Kingdom He came to establish was not one of earthly dominion. His disciples were to be brought before governors and kings, persecuted from city to city, delivered up by their own kin to death, and hated of all men for His Name's sake. And He explicitly said, "I am not come to send peace but a sword." The Kingdom of heaven, therefore, must be a Kingdom that is consistent with these prophecies of the Lord.

The words of John the Baptist, "Behold the Lamb of God which taketh away the sin of the world," also declare with unmistakable clearness the purpose for which He came into the world. Those words, moreover, are of the deepest significance. They connect directly with Abraham's prophetic saying in answer to Isaac's great question, "Where is the Lamb?"—to which Abraham responded, "My son, God will *provide Himself a lamb*" (Gen. 22:8). Here then, at last, was the "Lamb of *God*," come to offer the appointed Sacrifice. This one Scripture alone utterly excludes the idea that the Kingdom, in the sense foretold by the prophets and eagerly expected by the Jews, was or could have been within the purpose of the Lord's first coming.

The words, "Behold the Lamb of God" also connect with 1 Peter 1:18–20: "redeemed . . . with the precious blood of Christ, as of a Lamb without blemish and without spot; Who verily was foreordained *before the foundation of the world;*" also with Revelation 13:8: "the book of life of the Lamb slain from the foundation of the world." Those Scriptures show that the *sufferings* of Christ (and not His *glory*) were the purpose of His first coming, and that such was the plan of God from "before the foundation of the world."

In fact there is no supposition that could do greater violence to the most weighty and most important testimony of the Word of God than the supposition that Christ offered Himself as Israel's King at His first coming, and would then have ascended the throne, had Israel accepted His offer. There never was any such offer, nor any possibility of it. For such an offer, if accepted, would have nullified all those things which "*must* be" (as John 3:14; Matt. 16:21; Acts 17:3, etc.) in order that the Scriptures should be fulfilled. In a word, it would have set aside the Cross, and all that has eternally depended upon it.

The words, "Behold the Lamb of God which taketh away the sin of *the world,*" also connect with all those Scriptures which reveal the mighty fact that God's purpose in *this* age has to do, not with Israel only, but with the *whole world.* The very essence of the mysteries of the Kingdom of heaven is that "the field," occupied by that Kingdom, "is *the world*" (Matt. 13:38).

Further proof (if needed) that the Lord's purpose in coming into the world was to die on the cross—not to ascend the throne of David—is found in many of His own sayings, such as that "the Son of man came not to be ministered unto" (as *kings* are served) "but to minister, and to *give His life* a ransom for many" (Matt. 20:28). And we have, moreover, such Scriptures as Hebrews 10:5–10, showing in the plainest terms that He came into the world to do the Will of God by offering His body as a sacrifice for sins. Or, as stated in Hebrews 9:26, "Now once, in the end of the world (age) hath He appeared *to put away sin by the sacrifice of Himself.*" There could not be, and never could have been, any possibility of the earthly Kingdom of Christ, which the Old Testament prophecies foretell, until He should have "made *peace* by the blood of His Cross." The "sufferings" must of necessity precede the "glory."

The foregoing, and many other Scriptures, prove conclusively that Christ came into the world to die for sinners. Hence, when He announced the Kingdom of heaven, He had reference to something that was in perfect harmony with *that* purpose. Indeed, the Kingdom which He announced, and which He came to establish, depended upon His own death and resurrection.

But more than this, the preaching of the Kingdom continued *after* He was rejected by the rulers of Israel, *precisely the same as before.* There was no change, and no "withdrawal" of the Kingdom. The rejection of Christ is evidenced, we are told, in the events described in Matthew 11 and 12, when the Pharisees "held a council against Him, how they might destroy Him," and when they committed the unpardonable sin, saying, "This fellow doth not cast out devils but by Beelzebub, the prince of the devils" (Matt. 12:14, 24, 31, 32). Yet it was *after those events* that the Lord spoke the parables of the Kingdom of heaven; and He added other parables of the Kingdom from time to time thereafter, down to the very week of His death (Matt. 18:23; 20:1; 22:2; 25:1).

Moreover, as we have seen, the Lord in the same breath both announced to His disciples His approaching death, and also promised to Peter "the keys of the *Kingdom of heaven";* showing that the Kingdom of heaven was in perfect harmony with His death—in fact, that they are *directly linked together.* Again, still later, He declared that it was necessary for those He was addressing to be converted and become as little children in order to enter into the Kingdom of heaven (Matt. 18:3).

Referring to Luke's Gospel, we find that on the Mount of Transfiguration, Moses and Elias spoke with the Lord about "His decease which He should accomplish at Jerusalem" (Luke 9:31). And thereupon, the time being come "that He should be received up, He stedfastly set His face to go to Jerusalem" (verse 51). Yet *He did not cease to proclaim the Kingdom;* for, at verse 60 of the same chapter, He says to one who asked leave to go bury his father: "Let the dead bury their dead: but go thou and *preach the Kingdom of God.*" This Scripture alone affords conclusive evidence that the Kingdom that had been preached by John was not "withdrawn." But there is much more to the same effect.

In the next chapter we read: *"After these things* the Lord appointed other seventy also, and sent them forth to heal the sick and to say, The Kingdom of God is come nigh unto you" (Luke 10:1–9). In chapter 17:20, 21, He said to the Pharisees: "The Kingdom of God cometh not with observation . . . for behold, the Kingdom of God is within you" (*i. e.*, in the midst of, or among, you). In chapter 18:16, 17, He said: "Suffer little children to come unto Me, and forbid them not: for of such is the Kingdom of God. Verily I say unto you, Whosoever shall not receive the Kingdom of God as a little child shall in nowise enter therein." Thus it appears that He continued giving "the Word of the Kingdom" to the end of His days on earth. And not only so, but after His resurrection, He was seen of His disciples forty days, doing what? "Speaking of the things pertaining to the Kingdom of God."

Furthermore, after His ascension, when the disciples were scattered from Jerusalem and went everywhere "preaching the Word," it seems from what is said concerning Philip that they were "preaching the things concerning *the Kingdom of God* and the Name of Jesus Christ" (Acts 8:4, 12).

Not only so, but the Apostle Paul described his own ministry as "preaching the Kingdom of God" (Acts 20:25). It is recorded that in Ephesus he spoke in the synagogue for three months "persuading the things concerning *the Kingdom of God,*" and afterward "continued by the space of two years; so that all they which dwelt in Asia heard the word of the Lord Jesus, both Jews and Greeks" (Acts 19:8–10). This agrees with Paul's words in Acts 20:25, proving conclusively that the Gospel preached by him was the good news concerning the Kingdom of God. From these Scriptures it is evident that Paul at least was not aware that the Kingdom had been withdrawn, for he continued, to the end of his life, expounding, testifying, and preaching "*the Kingdom of God,*" to both Jews and Gentiles (Acts 28:23 and 31).

Thus it is made perfectly clear that there was no change whatever in the purpose of God for this age, or in the character of the preaching of Christ and His apostles, which was the same from first to last. The plan of God was carried out in every detail according to His determinate counsel and foreknowledge; and the Kingdom has exactly the place in this age which He intended that it should have "from the foundation of the world."

Not only is it quite widely taught that the Lord

Jesus offered Himself to the Jews as their King, and would have ascended the throne of David had they accepted His offer, but it is even said that the offer was renewed, after the Lord's ascension into heaven, by the mouth of the Apostle Peter; and we are told that had the Jews even then accepted the offer the Lord would have returned immediately from heaven, and would have taken the Kingdom.

As to this we would remark that, had Peter taken it upon himself to make such an offer as is attributed to him, he would have shown an extraordinary disregard of the commands which the Lord had given to His disciples in general, and to Peter in particular, by which they were required to bear witness to the risen Christ among all the nations of the earth. And moreover, he would have shown complete forgetfulness of all that Christ had foretold concerning themselves, and concerning Jerusalem,—forgetfulness that is unthinkable, now that the Holy Spirit had come to bring all Christ's sayings to their remembrance. For the Holy Spirit had come down from heaven, not to inspire such an "offer" as outlined above, but to empower the servants of Christ for their world-wide and age-long work of evangelization, and to quicken and indwell all who should receive by faith the "good seed" of the Word of God—the Gospel of Jesus Christ.

But the fact is that Peter made no such offer. And even if he had, we do not see how any mortal man could tell us what the Lord would have done had the supposed offer been accepted by the Jews. This "offer" is said to have been made in Peter's address, recorded in Acts 3:12–26, in the course of which he said:

> "Repent ye, therefore, and be converted, that your sins may be blotted out, when the times of refreshing shall come from the presence of the Lord, and He shall send Jesus Christ, which before was preached unto you, whom the heaven must receive until the times of restitution of all things which God hath spoken by the mouth of all His holy prophets since the world began."

There is, in the foregoing passage, no hint of any offer of Christ as King, much less is there any statement that He would return immediately and take the throne, if the Jews would accept the offer. On the contrary there is a plain declaration that "the heaven *must* receive 'Him' until the times of restitution"—which are not come yet.

It needs no great effort of mind to comprehend that Peter was calling upon his hearers for *individual* repentance and conversion, to the end that their individual sins might be blotted out, so that "times of refreshing *may* come," as indeed they *will* come, when the work of preaching "repentance and the forgiveness of sins" in the Name of Jesus Christ (Luke 24:47), has been completed. But the immediate restoration of the Kingdom to Israel is quite another matter, and was not so much as hinted at in Peter's address. There is no mention of either King or Kingdom in the entire discourse.

The above passage is rendered in Bagster's literal translation as follows:

> "Repent therefore and be converted for (or

unto) the blotting out of your sins. *So that* times of refreshing may come from the presence of the Lord."

The sense of the passage is quite plain.

It is safe to say that, in all God's plan, there is no such thing as the "offer" to Israel of Christ as their King, and no such thing as the taking up of His sovereign authority being dependent upon the caprice of men. When the appointed time comes, and not before, God will assuredly anoint His King upon Zion, the hill of God's holiness (Psa. 2:6); and the opposition of people and rulers will not avail to prevent it. Moreover, the conditions, as regards Israel, at the time when this purpose of God shall be carried out, are described in Zechariah 12:9–14. The people of Israel will not be consulted as to their choice in the matter. It is not for them to accept or decline their King when the moment comes for Him to take up His power and reign. "In that day," when their enemies are gathered against Jerusalem in overwhelming force, the Deliverer shall suddenly appear; and *they shall look on Him Whom they have pierced.* To the same effect another prophecy declares: "Behold He cometh with clouds, and every eye shall see Him, and *they also which pierced Him,* and all kindreds of the earth shall wail because of Him" (Rev. 1:7).

In accepting the speculative and utterly unfounded theory we have been discussing, one must assume the possibility that the foregoing prophecies, and scores of others besides, could be nullified, and that the whole scheme of Redemption, as revealed in the Scriptures, could be deranged. In fact, the acceptance of Peter's supposed offer and its supposed results, would have made it impossible that the New Testament Scriptures could ever have been written. All the history of God's work from Pentecost to the present day would have been changed, and even the Gospels would have been written differently, if at all.

And what does one gain by accepting these fancies, whereby—under the specious claim of "rightly dividing the Word of truth"—the entire plan of the ages is dislocated, and things which God has joined together (as the Church of Christ and the Kingdom of heaven) are put asunder? What profit is there in speculating as to what would have happened, if something else had happened, which in fact did not happen? We can see no profit or advantage in such imaginings. On the contrary, we see *much harm* therein. For, because of this, the Gospel of Matthew, and other portions of Scripture which are of *immediate application to God's people in this age*, have been neglected, and the words and commandments of Christ have been relegated to some other dispensation.

V

THE KINGDOM OF HEAVEN AND THE KINGDOM OF GOD

THE expression "Kingdom of heaven" occurs only in Matthew's Gospel. That Gospel, moreover, contains ten parables of the Kingdom of heaven, but three of which are repeated in other Gospels, where they are connected with the term "Kingdom of God." From these facts it is evident that Matthew's Gospel is intended to give special information in regard to the Kingdom of heaven; and hence we should make diligent effort to ascertain with certainty the significance of that expression. In our effort to do so we must learn to distinguish, when necessary, between "the Kingdom of heaven" and "the Kingdom of God." Generally they mean one and the same thing; but not always. Many statements that are made in Matthew concerning the Kingdom of heaven are made in other Gospels concerning the Kingdom of God. From this and other evidences we must conclude that the Kingdom of heaven *is* the Kingdom of God. But on the other hand, the Kingdom of God is *not always* the Kingdom of heaven. For the Kingdom of God is an expression of broad meaning. It embraces the sphere or realm of God's rule in whatever age or place. It is used of the age past, of the age now present, and of the age to come. Therefore it *embraces* the Kingdom of heaven, but is much broader. For the Kingdom of heaven is limited to *that peculiar form which God's Kingdom assumes in this present age.* The Kingdom of heaven begins at Pentecost and continues to the resurrection and rapture of the saints. It will be followed immediately by "the Kingdom of the *Son of man.*" The latter is also the Kingdom *of God,* but it is not the Kingdom of *heaven.*

The Kingdom of heaven was introduced into the world by preaching the Gospel (which is sowing the "good seed" of the Kingdom of heaven); and its outward form or character is such that the Lord has likened it to a field of ripening grain, with which "tares" are intermingled and allowed to grow to maturity. The Kingdom of the Son of man will be introduced with power, and *its* outward aspect will have all the appropriate displays of royal authority, power and glory. The appearance or "likeness" of the Kingdom will, until then, be such as is represented by the Lord's parables of the Kingdom of heaven, which we are about to examine. But at the end of this age will occur a sudden and marvellous transformation: for then the Lord Jesus shall be revealed from heaven with His mighty angels (the angels of His power) in flaming fire, taking vengeance on them that know not God, and that obey not the Gospel of our Lord Jesus Christ (2 Thess. 1:7, 8).

It follows that, when the expression "Kingdom

of God" occurs in the New Testament, it may mean either the Kingdom of *heaven* (the *present* form of God's Kingdom) as in Acts 19:8; 20:25; 28:23, 31; Romans 14:17; 1 Corinthians 4:20, and generally in the Gospels of Mark, Luke, and John; or it may mean the Kingdom of the Son of man (the future form of God's Kingdom) as in 1 Corinthians 6:9 and 15:50; Galatians 5:21; 2 Thessalonians 1:5; or it may mean the "law and the prophets" (the past form of God's Kingdom) as in Matthew 21:43.

The term "Kingdom of heaven" is a descriptive title, the significance of which lies in the fact that the Sovereign Ruler—the "King invisible" (1 Tim. 1:17)—is in heaven; of Whom the Apostle Peter said, "Whom *the heaven* must receive until the times of restitution" (Acts 3:21). The 110th Psalm foretells this period in the words: "The Lord said unto my Lord, Sit Thou at my right hand *until* I make Thine enemies Thy footstool." Until then we have the Kingdom of heaven, during which God is *reconciling* His enemies, not punishing them. The same Psalm also clearly announces the dispensation which is to succeed the Kingdom of heaven by telling what will happen in "the day of His wrath" (verses 5, 6).

In the Gospel of Matthew the expression "Kingdom of God" occurs five times; and from those passages we may find much help in our effort to distinguish the two expressions. Why, we may ask, does the Lord, in those few instances, use "Kingdom of God" instead of "Kingdom of heaven"? For example, in Matthew 6:33 we read: "Seek ye first the Kingdom of God." Why not "Kingdom of heaven"? Evidently the point of the Lord's teaching in this passage is that His disciples were to seek God's rule or authority in the broadest sense, and not merely that peculiar form of His Kingdom which was about to be introduced into the world.

In Matthew 12:28, where the Lord said: "But if I cast out devils by the Spirit of God, then *the Kingdom of God* is come unto you," the point evidently is that His casting out of demons was the exercise of the *authority of God.* The term "Kingdom of heaven" would plainly have been out of place here.

In Matthew 21:43, the Lord said to the Pharisees: "The *Kingdom of God* shall be taken from you and given to a nation bringing forth the fruits thereof"; and in this passage likewise the expression "Kingdom of heaven" would not have suited at all; for the Israelites never had *that* phase of the Kingdom. But in Matthew 23:13, again speaking to the Pharisees, the Lord said: "Ye shut up *the Kingdom of heaven* against men: for ye neither go in yourselves, neither suffer ye them that are entering to go in." Here we see clearly the appropriateness of the expression "Kingdom of heaven," for that was the special form of the Kingdom into which Christ was calling men by His preaching.

Of the six parables of the Kingdom recorded in Matthew 13, but one is found in Mark, the mustard-seed (chap. 4:30, 31), and but two in Luke (the mustard-seed and the leaven—chap. 13:18 and 20).

The most important parable of the Kingdom (the tares), and the three that give the inside view (the treasure, the pearl, and the drag-net) are found only in Matthew. Besides these, Matthew has four other parables of the Kingdom of heaven (18:23; 20:1; 22:1; 25:1).

The parable of the Sower, which is found in all three Gospels, is not called a parable of the Kingdom. It pictures (as we understand it) the *personal ministry* of the Lord Jesus Christ Himself among the Israelites, and the results of *that* ministry.

The first parable of the Kingdom of heaven—that of the tares of the field—is the most comprehensive and most characteristic of all: for it states definitely how and when *the Kingdom of heaven began,* and how and when it will *end.* And it states also what is the character of that Kingdom, from beginning to end. From it we learn that the Kingdom of heaven, which was announced by John Baptist and by the Lord as "at hand," actually began in the form it was to have in this age, with the preaching of the Gospel to "the world"—*i. e.,* to Jews and Gentiles alike, without distinction or difference. To Peter were promised the keys of the Kingdom of *heaven* (*not* the keys of the Kingdom of *God*—for his office was not so broad as that). Hence we find Peter opening the door of the Kingdom first to the Jews, at Pentecost, and afterwards to the Gentiles, at the house of Cornelius. From the work which the Lord appointed to Peter to do in connection with the "Kingdom of heaven," we can very definitely ascertain the precise significance of that expression.

The parable of the tares, or rather the Lord's explanation of it, also shows that the *Kingdom of heaven* will end with the end of this age (verse 40), for then will come "the harvest" or the gathering up of all the fruits of the labors of Christ's servants in the world during the age; and it will be followed by the Kingdom of the Son of man (verse 41). Then, the character of the Kingdom will be completely transformed: "The *Son of man* shall send forth His angels, and they shall gather out of *His* Kingdom all things that offend, and them that do iniquity."

We hope by the foregoing explanation (aided also by the discussion of the parables, which follows) to clear away from the minds of our readers all confusion as regards the meaning of the two expressions which we have been attempting to define. The existing confusion has been caused, in large part, by the fact that in current literature, printed for the benefit of the people of God, "the Kingdom" is usually viewed as *future,* and hence the word itself is commonly used to denote the coming millennial Kingdom of Christ. But in the New Testament, on the contrary, "the Kingdom of God" means *usually,* and "the Kingdom of heaven" means *always,* the *present phase* of the Kingdom, in the peculiar form it assumes from the time of Christ's ascension into heaven till His second coming.

The whole subject will become clarified when one grasps the simple fact that the "Kingdom," which was announced by John the Baptist, and by Christ and His Apostles, was not a *conditional offer* of God to emancipate the Jews and restore earthly dominion to the nation of Israel, which offer was withdrawn because the Jews would not accept their Messiah, but was a straightforward, unconditional announcement of the very same "Kingdom of heaven," which the Lord subsequently outlined in His parables of the Kingdom, and the very same Kingdom which Paul preached to the end of his days. That Kingdom of the "invisible" King, with its extraordinary "mysteries," was always in the purpose of God for this age. No other Kingdom ever was in His purpose for this age; nor is there the faintest suggestion, in the New Testament Scriptures, that any other Kingdom was contemplated or was announced by John the Baptist, or by Christ and His apostles.

Therefore we assuredly maintain that, when God did cause it to be announced that the Kingdom of heaven was "at hand," it *was* at hand; and that all that has occurred since that announcement has been strictly in accordance with "the determinate counsel and foreknowledge of God." For while the Kingdom which the Son of God came to introduce into the world was indeed the "Kingdom of God"—for it is of God and its citizens are "subject to the law of God" which the mind of the flesh is not, neither indeed *can* be (Rom. 8:7)—nevertheless, the form and character of that Kingdom are so extraordinary, so unlike any *earthly* Kingdom, and so different to the Kingdom foretold by the Old Testament prophets, that it was desirable to designate it *at first* by a special name. And inasmuch as Matthew's Gospel stands at the beginning of the

New Testament, and was manifestly given for the special purpose of laying the foundation for a correct understanding of God's work *in this present age*—which had been hidden from the view of the prophets of old—the distinctive titles "Kingdom of heaven" and Kingdom of "the Son of man" are given *only* in the first Gospel. And for the same reason, doubtless, we have *only in that Gospel* the complete line of Kingdom parables, the Sermon on the Mount, the complete commission to the disciples for their work in this age, and notably, the *only references to the Church.*

Hence, when viewed dispensationally, the Gospel of Matthew, which has been designated by some expositors as "Jewish," and assigned to some other age, is preëminently *the Gospel for this present dispensation,* which it bounds, defines, and explains.

But inasmuch as the new and wonderful Kingdom which the Lord announced is fully explained in the first Gospel, and is presumably understood by those for whose benefit the Scriptures are given, there is no need to designate that Kingdom in other portions of the New Testament by its special and distinctive name. Hence the invariable designation "Kingdom of God" in the other Gospels, and in the book of Acts, and the Epistles.

VI

PARABLES OF THE KINGDOM OF HEAVEN

ATTENTION should be given to the grouping of the seven parables of Matthew 13. That of the Sower stands by itself; and, besides being detached from the other six, it is not introduced, as they are, by the words, "The Kingdom of heaven is like . . ." It has a special prominence as the first of all the Lord's parables, and as being found in three of the Gospels, coupled in each case with the Lord's explanation of it. The extended comment upon it, recorded in Matthew 13:10–17, shows that it affords an example of the Lord's general purpose in making use of parables. The words of Mark 4:13 point clearly to the same conclusion: "And He said unto them, Know ye not *this* parable? And how then will ye know all parables?"

Israel's refusal to hear Christ and to receive His testimony, and to receive also the witness of John, and the witness of the works which the Father had given the Son to do, and the testimony also of their own Scriptures (John 3:11, 32; 5:32–39), had brought upon them the judgment foretold in Isaiah 6:9–13. Hence the Lord began to speak in a way which conveys the truth *only* to those whose hearts are not closed to His message.

The importance of what He is about to make known is immense. Many prophets and righteous men had longed to see and to hear those things, and it was denied to them. But "blessed" are they whose eyes have been opened to see, and their ears to hear, and their hearts to understand the precious things which the Lord here is bringing forth out of His treasure. His words should stimulate us to the utmost diligence in seeking to lay hold on these things.

The parable of the Sower apparently describes the Lord's personal ministry in Israel. He went forth as a Sower *to sow,* not as a King to conquer. The character of His ministry was foretold in Isaiah 61:1, 2; and He applied that prophecy to Himself: "He hath anointed Me to *preach the Gospel* to the poor" (Luke 4:18). This word of the Lord, spoken at the very beginning of His ministry, is quite evidence enough that He came as the anointed *Prophet,* to preach the Gospel, not as the anointed *King,* for the political deliverance of Israel.

A much older prophecy had said: "I will raise them up a Prophet . . . and will put My words in His mouth; and He shall speak unto them all that I shall command Him" (Deut. 18:18). In fulfillment of those prophecies, we have such descriptions of His ministry as these: "Jesus came into Galilee preaching the Gospel of the Kingdom." "And He said unto them, Let us go into the next towns that I may preach there also: for *therefore came I forth.*

And He preached in their synagogues throughout all Galilee" (Mark 1:14, 38, 39).

The parable of the Sower indicates also the *results* of His own ministry; and it would not be difficult to find in the Gospels illustrations of the four classes of hearers of His word. That the fourth class—the "good ground" hearers—was numerically small, notwithstanding the great multitudes that thronged to hear Him and to see His miracles, is evident from the sequel to His ministry.

The remaining six parables of Matthew 13 are divided into two groups of three each. The first group were spoken outside the house, in the hearing of the multitude. They give an *outward view,* so to speak, of what the Kingdom should be "like." After speaking them He sent the multitudes away and went into the house (verse 36). There He first explained to His disciples the parable of the tares of the field; and then He spoke, *to them only,* another group of three parables. These differ materially from the first three in that they show *what God gets* out of the world, as the result of the redemption-work of Christ; whereas the leading feature of the first three is the *working of evil* within the precincts of the Kingdom. Thus, the grouping of the parables is very instructive.

The Tares of the Field

This is the most comprehensive of the parables. It covers this entire age, thus giving a complete view of the "Kingdom of heaven" in its chief features from beginning to end. Here is spread before our eye a divinely-drawn prophetic word-picture, exhibiting what the Kingdom—announced and founded by the Lord Himself—should be "like" during all the time of His absence in heaven, that is, during the time He is seated at the right hand of God as foretold in Psalm 110. The place of the Throne during all that time is in heaven, not on earth.

It should be kept clearly in mind that we have here a *real Kingdom,* notwithstanding that the *pattern* of it is utterly unlike that of any other kingdom. The essence of a Kingdom is *rule,* or *government.* It is a realm within which the *will of the sovereign* is *law.* But, in other kingdoms, the will of the sovereign is *enforced,* and suitable administrative means and measures are provided to that end; whereas, in this "Kingdom of heaven," obedience is altogether *voluntary.* Those who are admitted to the Kingdom are called upon to obey *"from the heart."* The Gospel, which calls men into this heavenly Kingdom, is preached "for the obedience of *faith.*" As Paul says to the Roman believers: "Ye *were* the servants of sin, but ye have *obeyed from the heart* that form of doctrine which was delivered you" (Rom. 6:17). The laws of this Kingdom are written—not in statute books, nor in tables of stone—but in the heart, in fulfillment of the promise of God, "I will put My laws into their hearts, and in their minds will I write them" (Jer. 31:33; Heb. 10:16).

In this Kingdom there is *no visible King,* and no

display of royalty. There are no magistrates to try and punish transgressors, no police to preserve order and arrest wrong-doers, no army to protect the people and to fight against enemies, no court, no retinue, no taxes or tax-gatherers, no officials of any kind, no rank or titles, no upper classes, no social inequalities. In it there are no more outward displays of governmental authority than are seen in a field of ripening grain. Yet it is a *real Kingdom,* for all that. The law of this Kingdom is "the law of Christ" (Gal. 6:2); and the only power by which it is enforced is the *love* of Christ. "For the love of Christ constraineth us"—nothing else; and those who yield to that constraining power are they who *voluntarily* take His yoke upon them. They who have been set free by the Gospel of God from the bondage of sin, from the authority of Satan, and from the fear of death, are called upon to *yield themselves unto God,* as those that are alive from the dead, and their members as instruments of righteousness unto God (Rom. 6:13). But they are under *no compulsion.* Commandments from the One they confess as LORD have been given them; but they are not *forced* to yield obedience to them. The motive for obedience proceeds solely from the promptings of a heart that responds to His love, according as He Himself has said, "If ye *love Me,* keep My commandments." Forms, and rites, and ceremonies avail nothing in this Kingdom. "Circumcision is nothing, and uncircumcision is nothing, but keeping the commandments of God" (1 Cor. 7:19. Cf. 1 Cor. 14:37; 1 Thess. 4:2; 2 Pet. 3:2).

The essential characteristic of this Kingdom is *Grace,* which is manifested in freely forgiving others, in meekness, gentleness and forbearance toward all, in refraining from judgment, and in loving even our enemies. For Christ Himself became obedient unto death, to the end that, even "as sin had reigned unto death, even so might GRACE REIGN through righteousness, unto eternal life by Jesus Christ our Lord." The words just quoted from Romans 5:21 introduce important Kingdom-truth, which fills the sixth chapter of that Epistle.

Bearing in mind then the great fact that we have here a *real Kingdom,* though the King be "invisible"—(as Paul said, "Now unto the King, eternal, immortal, *invisible,* the only wise God, be honor and glory forever and ever"—1 Tim. 1:17)—let us note certain striking features of it, as pictured in the parable.

In the history of mankind, kingdoms have their rise in conquest, or in some social upheaval, or some political event, or in the successful scheming of an ambitious individual, or a party banded together for common advantage. But the Kingdom of heaven originated in a totally different manner, namely, by the *preaching* of a divine message, called "the Gospel." The power that gathers subjects for the Kingdom of heaven, and that qualifies them for admission into it, lies wholly in *the message itself.* It owes nothing whatever to the influence or ability of the men who carry the message. The first preachers of this message were men of no influence, learning, nor social position. The *Gospel itself* is "the power of God unto salvation." It acts in a manner similar to that of a seed cast into the ground. There, in the dark earth, hidden from view, where decay and corruption are in process, a new life springs up, a new creature is born and begins an existence as a living thing. So the "good seed" of the Word of God germinates in the hidden recesses of the corrupt human heart, and life "after its kind" springs into existence, "he knoweth not how" (Mark 4:27). This is the new birth which *must* take place before a man can enter into the Kingdom of God (John 3:3–6). For "the good seed are *the children of the Kingdom*" (Matt. 13:38).

The Apostle Peter speaks of this "holy nation," whom he also exhorts to be "as obedient children," reminding them that they had been "born again, not of corruptible seed, but of incorruptible, by the *Word of God* . . . and this is the *Word* which by *the Gospel* is preached unto you" (1 Pet. 1:14, 23–25; 2:9).

To the same effect the Apostle Paul writes to the believers at Colosse, concerning "the *word* of the truth of *the Gospel*, which is come unto you, as it is in all *the world;* and *bringeth forth fruit.*" And he shows that, by means of the Gospel, God "hath delivered us from the *power* (or authority) *of darkness,* and hath translated us into *the Kingdom of His dear Son*" (Col. 1:5, 6, 13). This gives precisely the same explanation of the effect of the Gospel that is given, pictorially, in the parable of the tares. The Gospel goes into "all the world" ("the field is the world"); and by its inherent power those who believe are liberated from the despotic servitude of sin—the authority of darkness—and are translated into a heavenly Kingdom, the Kingdom of the Son of God's love.

Thus the Kingdom of heaven is recruited by the working of God's mighty power, quickening dead sinners by means of the Gospel; yet the marvellous work attracts little or no attention in the world. It creates no more commotion than the springing up and the growth of a field of grain.

Yet this work, so little understood or valued by the world, is well understood by the "Wicked One," who is being despoiled of his goods. The Lord sent Paul, with the Gospel, to the nations of the earth, for this express purpose, namely, "to open their eyes, to turn them (the Gentiles) from darkness to light, and from *the power of Satan unto God*" (Acts 26:17, 18). Hence the "Enemy" is stirred to great activity. His enmity against the Seed of the woman, foretold in the first prophecy, now reveals itself. For in the parable it is stated that, after the "man" had sowed good seed in his field, "*his* enemy came and sowed tares." In view of the language of Genesis 3:15, which declares a special "enmity" between the serpent and the woman's "Seed" (the Son of man), the words "*his* enemy" are very significant. The form which this eternal "enmity" takes is one of the greatest of "the mysteries of the Kingdom." It will be considered later on.

VII

THE EXTENT AND DURATION OF THE KINGDOM OF HEAVEN

"The field is THE WORLD"

WE believe these few words have a much greater significance than is generally seen, and that they state one of the most important of those "mysteries" concerning this present age and its wonderful "Kingdom of heaven" that lay hidden in the counsels of God "from the foundation of the world"—a mystery which remained hidden until it was revealed by the Lord Jesus Christ in the simple words quoted above. For we have here the first announcement of the thrilling fact that the heavenly Kingdom, which the Lord came to announce and to introduce, was not to be confined to Judea, but was to embrace *the whole world.* It was to have no geographical boundaries whatever; for "the field is THE WORLD."

Accustomed as we now are to the preaching of Christ among all the nations, it requires an effort of mind to realize what an astonishing change it was in God's ways and dealings, that the heathen, with whom God's people had been forbidden even to eat, were to receive all the benefits of Christ's redeeming work on precisely the same terms as the Jews.

Nothing could have been more startling and revolutionary than the Lord's statement that: "Many shall come from the East and West, and shall sit down with Abraham and Isaac and Jacob in the Kingdom of heaven" (Matt. 8:11). *We* are used to thinking of Christianity as a great *Gentile* institution, to which an occasional Jew is admitted through the work of "Jewish missions." But just the reverse is the case. To *them*, as the Apostle Paul reminds us, that is, to the Jews—pertained "the adoption, and the glory, and the covenants"—the new as well as the old (see Jer. 31:31)—"and the service (of God) and the promises" (Rom. 9:4, 5). But, in the *hidden* purpose of God, we Gentiles were to share "the adoption, and the glory," and all the blessings of the new covenant. That was a great "mystery" or divine secret, which *now* is made known; for, to quote the Apostle Paul again: "the *Gentiles* have been made partakers of *their* (the Jews') spiritual things" (Rom. 15:27). It therefore behoves us, Gentiles, who, "being a wild olive tree," were "graffed in among them, and with them partake of the root and fatness of the Olive Tree," to take heed that we "boast not against the branches." For the Apostle of the Gentiles says: "But if thou boast, thou bearest not the root, but the root thee." "Be not high minded, but fear" (Rom. 11:17–20).

"The field is *the world.*" This is the first announcement of that fact to which the Apostle Paul so often referred with wonder, and in which he so greatly rejoiced. That ancient "middle wall of partition," which God Himself had erected between Jews and Gentiles, was now removed entirely and forever. And it required the death of the Lord Jesus Christ upon the cross to abolish it (Eph. 2:13–16). The preaching of salvation to "the world" was impossible until the Christ was first crucified and raised from the dead. Therefore, the Son of man "*must* be lifted up" (John 3:15, 16).

We have, then, the great fact that the preaching of Jesus Christ, whereby men are born again and whereby they enter the Kingdom of heaven, is as wide as *the world,* and that there is but one and the same Gospel for *all mankind.* "The Gospel of God concerning His Son, Jesus Christ our Lord" (Rom. 1:1–3), is sent into every country in the world, and to all classes of men. Such is the wonderful fact, once a "mystery" hidden even from God's prophets of old, but now revealed by the Lord in those few words, "the field is *the world,*" and further unfolded in later Scriptures of the New Testament.

God's *vineyard* of old, upon which He bestowed such care, and with such disappointing results, was the house of Israel, which occupied but an insignificant portion of the earth. "For the vineyard of the Lord of hosts is the *house of Israel,* and the men of Judah the plant of His delight" (Isa. 5:1–7). But now, in the new dispensation of the Gospel, God's *harvest-field* is "*the world,*" occupied by the depraved and idolatrous Gentiles. Such being the case, and it having seemed good to the Lord to choose and qualify a special messenger, the Apostle Paul, to preach the Gospel among the Gentiles, we should expect to find, in the ministry of Paul, special references to those "mysteries" which the Lord Jesus revealed in His parables. And that is just what we do find; for Paul has much to say about "the mysteries of God" of which he, and those associated with him in the ministry, were "stewards" (1 Cor. 4:1). Indeed, he is the only one of the New Testament writers who mentions them,—at least under the term "mysteries." And the chiefest of all those "mysteries of God," the one which Paul most frequently mentions, and always with wonder and delight, is that Christ, in all the fullness of His unsearchable riches, was "according to the commandment of the everlasting God," preached to *Gentiles,* on an exact equality with *Jews,* although Christ had been promised to Jews only.

As we read the various passages in which Paul speaks of the "mysteries of God," we will find that the fact to which he gives the greatest prominence is the same fact which the Lord Himself declared in the words "the field is the world," namely that "the *Gentiles* should be *fellow-heirs,* and of the *same body,* and *partakers* of His (God's) *promise in Christ,* by the *Gospel.*" This he calls "the mystery of Christ" (Eph. 3:3–8).

Bearing this in mind, we can see clearly the meaning of such passages as Romans 16:25, 26: "Now to Him that is of power to stablish you according to *my gospel and the preaching of Jesus Christ according to the revelation of the mystery,* which was *kept secret* since the world began, but now is made manifest, and by the Scriptures of the prophets (lit., by prophetic writings, meaning the New Testament Scriptures), according to the commandment of the everlasting God, made known to *all nations* for the obedience of faith."

Manifestly, "the preaching of Jesus Christ according to the revelation of the mystery, which *was* kept secret since the world began, but now is *made manifest,"* is simply the preaching of Christ "to *all nations"*; and that preaching is "for the obedience of faith," which is equivalent to saying that they who believe are made subject to the law of God, or in other words are *brought into the Kingdom of God.* It is quite clear that "the mystery which was *kept secret since the world began,"* of which Paul writes, is the same mystery which the Lord referred to as having been *"kept secret from the foundation of the world."*

The fullest explanation of this mystery—to wit, the sharing by believing Gentiles in all the fullness of Christ, and on terms of perfect equality with believing Jews, is found in Paul's Epistle to the Ephesians. The great theme of that Epistle is "the eternal *purpose"* of God "which He *purposed* in Christ Jesus our Lord" (3:11), namely, to choose a people *from among Gentiles* as well as Jews, forming *one body* in Christ. That purpose was formed "before the foundation of the world" (1:4), and Paul speaks of it as "the *mystery* of His Will, according to His good pleasure which He hath *purposed* in Himself" (1:9). The prominent subject of chapter 2 is that *Gentiles,* who were dead in trespasses and sins, and who, moreover, had no share whatever in the covenants of promise, having *no* hope, and without God in the world, had been "made nigh" to God in Christ Jesus, by His blood. "For through Him," says Paul, "we both (*i. e.*, both Jews and Gentiles) have access by one Spirit unto the Father." And he continues, "*Now* therefore, ye (Gentiles) are no more strangers and foreigners, but fellow-citizens with the saints (Israelites) and of the household of God."

It is easy to see that Paul, in this chapter, is simply unfolding that marvellous "mystery of God," namely, His previously hidden purpose with regard to believing Gentiles, which the Lord Himself briefly declared when He uttered the words "the field is the world."

In chapter 3 of Ephesians, Paul continues to dwell upon this subject of the place "in Christ" now given to believing Gentiles. When that chapter is read with an understanding of what the subject is, it not only becomes luminously clear, but also overflows with blessed and consoling truth for Gentiles who believe in Jesus Christ.

To those Ephesian believers (who were "Gentiles in the flesh," though "saints" in Christ Jesus), Paul speaks of "the dispensation of the grace of God which is given me to you-ward" (verse 2), referring to his special commission to preach Christ to Gentiles, and to this he again refers in rapturous terms in verse 8, saying: "Unto me, who am less than the least of all saints, is this grace given, that I should preach *among the Gentiles* the unsearchable riches of Christ."

And furthermore it was given to him, as he says in the next verse, "to make all men see what is *the fellowship of the mystery,* which *from the beginning of the world hath been hid in God.*" Fellowship means a sharing together, or having something in common; and the "fellowship of the mystery" is the sharing together by believing Gentiles equally with believing Jews, of "the unsearchable riches of Christ." That is the mystery of sowing the good seed of the Gospel of Christ in *all the world;* and Paul here repeats again the fact, which the Lord Himself first made known, that, though this mystery had not been revealed to the prophets of old, it had nevertheless lain in God's purpose "from the beginning of the world." To strengthen this statement, Paul declares that the great work of God to which he had been called (preaching the Gospel to Gentiles) was "according to *the eternal purpose* which He purposed in Christ Jesus our Lord . . . which is *your glory.*"[1]

Here, again, is declared the amazing and most blessed fact that, hidden in the counsels of God from the very beginning, lay the "purpose" to bring believers *from among the nations of the whole world,* into "glory." What is involved in that word "glory" is nothing less than the fullness of the blessing of Christ's millennial reign. (See last chapter of this book.)

Paul tells the Ephesians that the Lord Himself

[1] There is no doubt, I think, that the antecedent of "which is your glory," at the end of verse 13, is "the eternal *purpose*" of verse 11, the intermediate words being parenthetical. Obviously "your glory" could not refer to Paul's tribulations.

had "by revelation made known" to him "the mystery," of which he had written "in few words" in chapter 1, "whereby," he says, "when ye read ye may understand my knowledge in the *mystery of Christ,* which in other ages was not made known unto the sons of men, as it is now revealed unto His holy apostles and prophets by the Spirit" (verses 3–5). Paul had the knowledge of this important mystery by direct revelation, and not through other apostles or New Testament prophets, though they all had the knowledge as well as he. The frequent repetition of the statement that the mystery in question was hidden during the past ages of time, indicates the importance of that fact in God's eyes. It shows, among other things, that although God for a season "gave them up," *i. e.,* the Gentiles (Rom. 1:24, 28), He nevertheless had a fixed purpose of unspeakable blessing and privilege for them in Christ Jesus.

In verse 6 of Ephesians 3, Paul gives so clear a definition of this mystery as to leave little room for misunderstanding. The definition is as follows: "That *the Gentiles* should be *fellow-heirs* (*i. e.,* fellow-heirs with Jews), and of the *same body,* and *partakers* of His (God's) promise *in Christ";* and that this was to be accomplished "by (means of) *the Gospel."*

The literal rendering of Bagster's interlinear New Testament is very plain and forceful: "That the nations were to be joint-heirs, and a joint-body, and joint-partakers of His promise in the Christ, through the Gospel."

Manifestly, this is merely a detailed statement

of what the Lord revealed in the parable of the tares.

Again, in Colossians 1:25–27, Paul speaks of the "dispensation of God" that had been given him "for *you*" (Gentiles) "to fulfill the Word of God"; and explains that the special Word of God which he had been charged to fulfill was "the *mystery* which hath been *hid* from ages and from generations, but now is made manifest to His (God's) saints, to whom God would make known what is the riches of the glory of this *mystery among the Gentiles;* which is *Christ among you,* the hope of glory."[1]

Preaching Christ among the Jews as their hope of glory would not have been a "mystery" at all; but the proclamation of the Messiah, or Christ, among *Gentiles,* as *their* "hope of glory," was a startlingly new thing in apostolic days. For Gentiles were "without Christ," having "no hope" (Eph. 2:12).

Again, we refer our readers to the last chapter of this book for the significance of the word "glory," which occurs so frequently and so prominently in these Scriptures.

In Colossians, as in Ephesians, Paul shows that it is by *preaching the Gospel "in all the world"* (see Col. 1:5, 6, 23) that he executed the dispensation of God committed to him with regard to the "mystery" which had been revealed to him. This statement also connects Paul's ministry directly with that which the Lord outlined in the parable of the tares.

[1] The preposition "en" rendered "among," where it occurs before "Gentiles" is repeated before "you," and should obviously be rendered "among" there also.

The importance that Paul attached to his ministry is further indicated by his request to the Ephesians that they should pray for him that utterance might be given him to open his mouth boldly "to *make known the mystery of the Gospel*" (Eph. 6:19, 20).

Again Paul speaks in 1 Timothy 3:16 of the "mystery," which he here calls "the mystery of godliness." We have no difficulty in identifying this as the same mystery which he variously calls "the mystery of God," "the mystery of Christ," "the mystery of the Gospel." In chapter 1:11, of 1 Timothy, Paul speaks of the "glorious Gospel of the blessed God," which had been committed to his trust, which he defines as a "faithful saying and worthy of all acceptation," namely, "that Jesus Christ came into *the world* to save sinners" (verse 15); and then he ascribes "unto the KING, eternal, immortal, INVISIBLE, the only wise God, honor and glory forever and ever" (verse 17). In chapter 3:16 we have the familiar words in which the foundation truth of the Gospel is stated with such impressive power: "And without controversy great is the *mystery of godliness:* God was manifest in the flesh, justified in the Spirit, seen of angels, *preached unto the Gentiles,* believed on *in the world,* received up into (or, literally, *in*) *glory.*"

It is unnecessary to point out the correspondence between this Scripture and the parable of the tares; for it is apparent at a glance.

In all these Epistles of Paul, whom Christ specially

chose to preach Him among the Gentiles according to the revelation of the long-hidden purpose of God, and in whom Christ wrought by word and deed "to make *the Gentiles obedient*" (Rom. 15:18), we find, first, the dispensation of the Gospel committed to his trust, whereby men are "begotten" again (1 Cor. 4:15), and then we find *commandments of the Lord*, to be "obeyed from the heart" by those who have been brought, by the new birth, into the Kingdom of God. Although no force is used in this Kingdom, yet the Scriptures testify, in passages without number, that consequences of the most serious nature depend upon the obedience which we, "the children of the Kingdom," render to the commandments of Christ, whether given directly by Himself, or indirectly through His apostles. Our present purpose, however, is mainly to point out the close connection between the ministry of Paul and the "mysteries" revealed by the Lord Jesus Christ in His parables of the Kingdom of heaven. There has been widely spread in these days, and with unhappy consequences, a certain so-called "dispensational" teaching, to the effect that between the Lord's ministry of "kingdom-truth" (as it is called) and Paul's ministry of "church-truth," there is a great difference: whereas the fact is, and it is writ large upon the page of Scripture, that Paul's ministry is preëminently the ministry of the Kingdom of God in the exact character which God has given it in this age, according to the "mysteries" revealed by the Lord Jesus in His parables; and that Paul's ministry connects directly with, and carries forward, that of the Lord Jesus Christ. (See, for example, Rom. 15: 8, 9, and cf. Matt. 12: 17–21.)

The "Mystery" of Blinded Israel. In the Lord's discourse in Matthew 13, He made known a matter concerning the spiritual state of Israel during this age which runs parallel to the mystery of preaching the Gospel among the nations of the world. In regard to the mass of the Israelites, the Lord declared that, in fulfillment of Isaiah's prophecy (Isa. 6: 9–10), their hearts had become gross, their ears dull of hearing, and their eyes closed. This condition of the Israelites, and their attitude toward Christ and the Gospel, continues to the present day. But, from verse 13 of Isaiah 6, it is evident that there is to be a future restoration for them.

Paul takes up in Romans 11: 25 this feature of the Lord's discourse. The whole passage has to do with the grace of God extended in this age to *Gentiles,* who are regarded as occupying, for the time being, the place of privilege which naturally belongs to Israel. This fact of mercy to the Gentiles, during a period of time in which Israel is temporarily hardened, is represented, in Romans 11, under the figure of an olive tree, whose "natural branches" (Israelites) are broken off, and the branches of a wild olive tree (Gentiles) are graffed in "contrary to nature." And Paul makes known that this state of things is to continue throughout his age, saying: "For I would not, brethren, that ye should be ignorant of *this mystery,* lest ye should be wise in your own conceits; that *blindness* in part is happened to Israel until the *fullness of the Gentiles be come in.* And *so* all Israel shall be saved: as it is written, There shall come out of Zion the Deliverer, and shall turn away ungodliness from Jacob."

Here again is a clear statement touching this present age, which in times past was hidden in God's counsels, and during which He should be occupied in visiting the Gentiles, while Israel should be temporarily displaced from the position of favor.

There are other "mysteries," or facts, concerning this present age, facts hidden in the days of old, which the Lord first declared in His parables of the Kingdom and which His apostle Paul afterward developed in his inspired writings. Those further "mysteries" will be the subject of following chapters. Thus far we have dwelt upon the most prominent feature of this age, namely, the preaching among the outcast and abhorred Gentiles—the uncircumcised and the unclean—of "the unsearchable riches of Christ." That being the great outstanding "mystery" and marvel of God's amazing grace, we should not be surprised to find the whole subject of the Kingdom dealt with fully and in detail by that man (the Apostle Paul) who was specially chosen by "the King invisible" to carry on the foreordained work among the Gentiles. This is one of the marvellous harmonies of God's wonderful Word, notwithstanding that heretofore it seems to have been generally overlooked.

VIII

"HIS ENEMY CAME"—THE MYSTERY OF INIQUITY

ONE of the most extraordinary facts about the Kingdom of heaven, as pictured in the parable of the tares of the field, is the work which the devil is permitted to do, unopposed and unhindered, within the domain of the Kingdom. That God would ever give the devil such a free hand was surely a "mystery"; but we can easily see now that, precisely as the Lord foretold in the parable and in His explanation of it, so it has been to this day. The devil's work still goes on, and the results of *his* sowing are allowed to ripen "till the harvest."

The "enmity," foretold in the first prophecy of the Bible, between the Seed of the woman and the seed of the wicked one, takes a very peculiar form in this age. It is evident that the enemy is not permitted to uproot a single blade of wheat in all the field, so he resorts to the expedient of sowing tares among the wheat. This is done by stealth, "while men slept," as it were by night. In other words, it is accomplished in such a way that *the enemy's hand in the matter is concealed.* The servants of the householder are unable to account for the presence of tares, where "good seed" had been sown. From this we understand that the seed which the devil sows bears a deceitful resemblance to the good seed;

also that the devil's ministers, by whom his seeds are sown, have free access to "the field," and are able to pass, in the eyes of "men," as the ministers of righteousness.

In all the particulars noted above, the Lord's prophetic parable has been marvellously fulfilled. Let it be observed, in the first place, that the "tares" are not mere "professors," that is to say, unconverted persons who are nominally "Christian," and who are often found in company with believers. Such are not necessarily "the children of the wicked one." Merely unconverted persons, or formal "professors," are never called, in Scripture, "children of the devil." That name is reserved for those who are *active enemies of the truth,* being energized in a direct way by the Spirit of Evil, even as the children of God are energized by the Spirit of God. (See Acts 13:10.)

The "children of the Wicked One" are men who *receive, believe in, and become animated by, satanic lies.* They are the direct and inevitable product of a *sowing* of satanic *doctrines,* just as children of God are the product of the preaching of Christ. So we have, in this part of the Lord's parable, a foretelling of the remarkable fact that, in all parts of the world where the Gospel has *first* been preached (*and only in such parts*), there have appeared energetic, zealous and enterprising men, actively sowing doctrines from which have sprung up (not masses of mere "professors" or indifferent hearers, but) multitudes of *earnest devotees of falsehood,* persons who are most ardently attached to the doctrines they have received, most zealous in defending and spreading them, and ready to suffer for them if need be. The "children of the wicked one," begotten of satanic lies, are very different indeed from the ordinary masses who make a mere formal profession of Christianity.

And not only so, but the false and poisonous doctrines thus introduced among believers bear a deceitful resemblance to "the doctrine of Christ." Men in general are completely deceived; and even "the elect" need to exercise care in order to distinguish the spurious Gospels from the true "Gospel of God." Thus the devil has wrought from the very beginning of the Kingdom of heaven, "with all deceivableness of unrighteousness in them that perish" (2 Thess. 2:9, 10). From the outset the Apostles gave warnings of these activities of the enemy. Paul warned the Corinthians of those who should come preaching "*another Jesus* whom we have not preached," and warned them also against receiving "*another spirit* whom ye have not received, or *another gospel* which ye have not accepted" (2 Cor. 11:4). Wherever "the Gospel of God concerning His Son" has been preached, there has followed the preaching of "another Jesus," one who is not "God over all and blessed forevermore" (Rom. 9:5), but a mere "reformer," a great "teacher," a "leader and example" among men; and "another spirit," not the Holy Spirit of God Who is "*given*" to believers in Jesus Christ; and "another gospel," in which there is no redemption by blood, no risen Saviour, no power of God unto salvation to every one that believeth.

Such were the Arians, Socinians and Gnostics of early days, and such are the present-day "Mormons," "Christadelphians," and certain sects of "Adventists" who deny the Deity of the Lord Jesus Christ; also the followers of Mrs. Eddy and of "Pastor" Russell. These zealous devotees of "damnable heresies" are the fruit of the positive preaching of error, the industrious sowing of poisonous seeds, and are not the results merely of an indifferent hearing of the true Gospel. These deluded persons are so completely possessed by the "spirit of error" as to be utterly incapable of discerning the Truth. And the astonishing feature of the case is that the doctrines they have received, and *which have made them what they are,* are spread *in the name of Christ,* and upon the claim of Bible authority. Such are the "tares" and they who receive them.

Another point of correspondence between prediction and fulfillment is seen in the fact that the agents of the devil, who spread these poisonous doctrines, are everywhere accepted by *the world* (and "the field is the world") as ministers of Christianity; and those who receive their doctrines are regarded by the world as "Christians." In this, again, we are reminded of Paul's warning regarding "false apostles, deceitful workers, transforming themselves into the apostles of Christ." "And no marvel," he says, "for Satan himself is transformed into an angel of light. Therefore it is no great thing if his ministers also be transformed as the ministers of righteousness, whose end shall be according to their works" (2 Cor. 11:13-15).

The disguised ministers of Satan, who spread his deadly falsehoods, are not distinguished, in the eyes of the world, from the "ministers of righteousness." This is everywhere apparent, and is one of the remarkable "mysteries of the Kingdom." But both in the parable, and in the Scripture just quoted, there is a pointed reference to the "end" of those wicked ministers of Satan and their deluded followers. The end will not come through any gradual weakening of the enemy's power and activity, or by any gradual triumph of right over wrong, or in any gradual betterment of the world. According to the parable, there is to be no check to the operations of the enemy, and no attempt at uprooting the tares in order to give better opportunity for the wheat to mature. A strange "kingdom" this, where a free hand is allowed to the enemy! This is, indeed, a "mystery." The command given by the Lord of the harvest is: "Let both grow together until the harvest." Both grain and tares are to have *precisely the same opportunity to grow.* Both are to receive the benefit of the same rain, the same sunshine, the same nourishment from the soil. Attempts to uproot the tares (as by violent attacks upon these teachers of error) are not only wasted efforts, but are contrary to the word "let both *grow.*" It would even seem that the more such systems as that of Mrs. Eddy and "Pastor" Russell are attacked, the more they flourish. And the result will be, as might be expected, that the noxious weeds will thrive amazingly as the time of harvest draws near. All Scripture bears witness to this. The Lord said:

"For there shall arise false Christs, and false prophets, and shall show great signs and wonders; insomuch that, if it were possible, they shall deceive the very elect" (Matt. 24:24). Paul says: "Now the Spirit speaketh expressly that *in the latter times* some shall depart from the faith, giving heed to seducing spirits and doctrines of demons" (1 Tim. 4:1). And again: "But evil men and seducers shall wax worse and worse, deceiving and being deceived" (2 Tim. 3:13). To the same effect the Apostle Peter says: "There shall be false teachers among you who *privily*" (cf. the words "while men slept") "shall bring in damnable heresies, even denying the Lord that bought them, and bring upon themselves swift destruction. And many shall follow their pernicious ways; by reason of whom the way of truth shall be evil spoken of" (2 Pet. 2:1, 2).

But there is a fixed limit to the period of God's tolerance of evil in the world. These things are to be allowed only "until the harvest." Then what a change will come over the scene where the good seed has been sown and where it has been ripening all through this long age! As in a field of grain the long, tranquil and comparatively uneventful period of growth and ripening of the plants is suddenly succeeded by a short season of great activity, even "*so* shall it be in the end of this age." The reapers will *first* gather together the tares and bind them in bundles for convenience in subsequently burning them (verse 30). "The reapers are the angels." Those invisible messengers of God, who are "great in strength," and who hearken "to the voice of His word," will, in some manner not explained, cause the children of the wicked one to be gathered closely together in federations, sects and societies, or the like, ready first for the convenient removal of the wheat, which is to be gathered into the barn; and second, for the consuming fires of the great tribulation and of the wrath to come.

The Mystery of Iniquity. At this point, we bring to mind Paul's prophecy concerning "the mystery of iniquity," which is clearly the same mystery of Satan's unhindered working within the precincts of the Kingdom, as foretold by the Lord in the parable of the tares. In 2 Thessalonians, chapters 1 and 2, Paul foretells the coming of the Lord when He shall be *revealed from heaven* with His mighty angels (lit., the angels of His strength) in *flaming fire* (chap. 1:7–9). This is the *final scene* of the short period of harvest at the end of the age. The wheat has previously been removed from the field (as, of course, the farmer's first thought is for his precious grain; and he would not think of setting fire to the rubbish until the grain is all gathered); and now the *angels* and *the flaming fire,* which figure so prominently in the parable, are employed for the "everlasting destruction" of the tares, even as described in the parable. Regarding the precise sequence of events at the time of the end, we will speak more definitely in the next chapter.

At this point we merely wish to show the culmination of Satan's work throughout this age. Of that work Paul says: "For the mystery of iniquity *doth already work*" (2:7). So we have here a further and a distinct statement that the work of the enemy began in apostolic times. "Only he who hinders will hinder until he be taken out of the way. And *then* shall that Wicked (one) be revealed."

From this we learn of something or some one *hindering* the final act of the great drama, the destruction of Antichrist ("that Wicked one"), who will appear at the very end of this age, and "whom the Lord shall consume with the spirit of His mouth, and shall destroy with the brightness of His coming." Likewise, in the parable, there is a cause which hinders the rooting up and destruction of the tares. But, at the appropriate time, the hindering cause *"will be taken out of the way."* In the parable, what hinders is *the presence of the wheat in the field.* But, when the wheat shall have been stored in the granary, that is to say, when all the children of the Kingdom shall have been "caught up together to meet the Lord in the air" (1 Thess. 4:16, 17), then "the field" will be cleared for the free action of the fires of tribulation and wrath.

Finally, we have only to notice that, in speaking of "the mystery of iniquity," Paul states that it is "the working of Satan," and that it is accomplished by lying and deceiving, "with all power and signs and lying wonders, and with all *deceivableness* of *unrighteousness* in them that perish; because they received not the love of *the truth*" (*i. e.*, the Gospel of Christ) "that they might be *saved.* And for this cause God will send them *strong delusion* that they should believe a lie" (lit., *the* lie).

This corresponds precisely with the parable of the

tares; and it accounts for the astonishing spread of "strong delusion" in these last days—such as so-called "Christian Science." And there is one point worthy of very special notice; namely, in the parable we see that the tares are sown *only* where the good seed has previously been sown. Hence those who fall a prey to Satan's delusions are those who *first had an opportunity to accept Jesus Christ as their Saviour*. They *might have* "received the love of *the Truth*," which the Gospel offers them, "that they might be *saved*." But "*because they received not*," but *rejected* the Son of God, Who died that sinners "might be saved," *therefore*, "*for this cause*" God gives them over to strong delusion, that they should believe *the lie*. Doubtless every one who accepts these "doctrines of demons" has *first* heard and refused to believe "the Gospel of God concerning His Son."

May none who read these lines refuse Him Who is *God's Salvation to the end of the earth* (Isa. 49:6) and thus expose himself to the awful peril of Satan's strong delusion. For "neither is there *salvation* in any other (except in Jesus Christ); for there is none other Name under heaven given among men, whereby we must be *saved*" (Acts 4:11).

IX

THE MYSTERY OF GOD FINISHED

"And the Angel sware by Him that liveth forever and ever . . . that there shall be time (delay) no longer, but in the days of the voice of the seventh angel, when he shall begin to sound, the *Mystery of God* should be *finished*, as He hath declared (lit., hath told the glad tidings) to His servants the prophets."

IT remains for us to speak of one more feature of "the mysteries of the Kingdom of heaven," as set before us in the wonderful parable of the tares of the field. That feature is of the deepest interest, for it concerns the final disposition of "the wheat." In the parable, when the servants—anxious and perplexed at the presence of tares (how many servants of the Lord have been needlessly perplexed by this, and have wasted time and strength in trying to root up the tares!)—asked the householder if they should go and gather them up, he tells them how he will deal with them "in the time of the harvest." For then he will say to the reapers, "Gather ye together *first* the tares to burn them"; and then he adds "but gather the wheat into my barn" (Matt. 13:30). Taking this in connection with the explanation found in verses 39–43, we can clearly establish the following sequence of events, which also is in accord with all other pertinent Scriptures. "The time of harvest" will be characterized, first, by divinely sent agencies, which will have the effect of gathering "the children of the wicked one" closely together. How far this process has already advanced we cannot say definitely. But while it is going on, at some day and hour known only to the Father (Mark 13:32), "the children of the Kingdom" will be taken away from the world, as foretold in the words "but gather the wheat into my barn," and as also is plainly declared in other Scriptures cited below. Then, the field being cleared of what is the Lord's, and only the "tares" remaining, along with unconverted people,—many of whom, however (that is, of the unconverted persons), will be saved through the great tribulation, as we shall see later on—the Antichrist, "that Wicked," will be revealed, and iniquity will reach its climax when he shall "exalt himself above all that is called God, or that is worshipped" (2 Thess. 2:4). This will bring on the great tribulation (Matt. 24:21; Rev. 7:14), followed by the day of "vengeance," at which time the tares will be burned in the fire, when the Lord shall be revealed from heaven, destroying Antichrist by the very brightness of His appearing. The angels will then gather out of His Kingdom every offensive thing and those who do iniquity. "And *then* shall the righteous," that is, the Lord's people, who will have returned to earth "with Him" (1 Thess. 4:14; Col. 3:4), "*shine forth* as the sun in the Kingdom of their Father."

This feature of the mysteries of the Kingdom is unfolded by the Apostle Paul in 1 Corinthians 15. The connection of that chapter with the parable of the tares of the field is clearly seen in the fact that it takes up the subject of the harvest. In an earlier chapter Paul had made known to the Corinthian believers (and with them to "*all* that in *every place* call upon the Name of the Lord Jesus Christ") the fact that they were "God's husbandry," or tillage, and that he, together with Peter, Apollos and others, were merely laborers in the field (3:5–9). But the fifteenth chapter carries us to the harvest-time, showing how the Lord will proceed to gather the precious fruits of the earth, for which He has waited long. First, Paul tells us that Christ Himself, risen from the dead, is the "First-fruits" of the great harvest (Christ's resurrection, on the first day of the week, "the morrow after the Sabbath," coincided with the Feast of First-fruits, when the sheaf of first-ripe grain was brought and waved before the Lord, Lev. 23:9–11); and "afterward they that are Christ's *at His coming*" shall be raised. Then, as regards the questions "*How* are the dead raised up? and *with what body* do they come?" he points to that which happens when a kernel of grain, such as wheat, is sown in the ground. God gives it a body "as it hath pleased Him." Then, after stating important facts concerning the resurrection, upon which facts we do not now stop to comment, he takes us directly to *the event itself*, saying: "Now this I say, brethren, that flesh and blood cannot inherit the Kingdom of God, neither doth corruption inherit incorruption."

Thus, at this point, the Kingdom of God is brought into view, which is another link with the parables of Matthew 13. And now come the important words: "Behold, I show you a *mystery;* we shall not all sleep, but we shall all be changed, in a moment, in the twinkling of an eye, at the last trump: for the trumpet shall sound, and the dead shall be raised incorruptible, and we shall be changed" (verses 50–52). Here we have a wonderful fact never before revealed—a "mystery." It is comparatively easy to understand that the dead, when raised, will receive bodies of glory, immortal and incorruptible. But how about those believers who are alive, in mortal bodies, at the time of the Lord's return? Must they suffer sudden death, in order to have part in the resurrection? Not so: "we shall *not all sleep*" the sleep of death; "but we shall *all be changed*"; and the change will be effected *in a moment,* even in the *twinkling of an eye.* And this expressly applies to *all* who are Christ's. *All* the living ones shall be changed in a moment at the last trump. Not one will be left to endure the awful sufferings of the great tribulation.

It will be clearly seen how this important revelation, given us through the Apostle Paul, coincides with and corroborates the sequence of events found in the parable, where the wheat, without exception, is gathered into the barn.

And now we turn to 1 Thessalonians 4:13–17 for further corroboration and for a further detail of great importance. We quote the entire passage:

> "But I would not have you to be ignorant, brethren, concerning them which are asleep, that ye sorrow not, even as others which have no hope. For if we believe that Jesus died and rose again, even so them also which sleep in Jesus will God bring with Him. For this we say unto you by the Word of the Lord, that we which are alive and remain unto the Coming of the Lord shall not prevent (precede) them which are asleep. For the Lord Himself shall descend from heaven with a shout, with the voice of the archangel, and with the trump of God; and the dead in Christ shall rise first; then we which are alive and remain shall be caught up together with them in the clouds, to meet the Lord in the air; and so shall we ever be with the Lord."

In 1 Corinthians 15, the question was mainly in regard to those who should be alive at the Lord's return. In 1 Thessalonians 4, the question is concerning them which are asleep. The two Scriptures taken together give complete information as to the disposition to be made of the Lord's people when the end of the age arrives. At some point in the indefinite period called "the *time* of the harvest," "the *end* of the age," "the last days," etc., the Lord will come to "the air," and at His summons or word of command ("shout"), the sleeping saints will rise incorruptible, and then, instantly, "in the twinkling of an eye," the living saints will be changed as to their bodies, "this mortal putting on immortality," and both together will be caught up to meet the Lord in the air. So we shall ever thereafter be with the Lord, and shall return "with Him" after the great tribulation is over (verse 14).

The two Scriptures, which thus reveal the main features of the gathering of the wheat into the granary, leave no room at all for the idea that only a select company of believers ("overcomers," as some say) will be raised and caught away to meet the Lord. Moreover, these Scriptures, with all others that refer to the Lord's coming *for* His people, make no mention at all of the great tribulation, thus corroborating what we have already pointed out,—namely, that the great tribulation, when the tares are consumed, occurs during the interval when the saints are with the Lord "in the air." At the end of the tribulation, the Lord will be "manifested" in glory, with His mighty angels, as already pointed out in connection with 2 Thessalonians, chapters 1 and 2. The "appearing," or *manifestation* of Christ, is spoken of in other Scriptures, such as Colossians 3:4: "When Christ, Who is our life shall *appear* (lit., be manifested, or revealed openly) then shall *ye also appear* (*be manifested*) *with Him in glory.*"

The Scripture quoted at the head of this chapter (Rev. 10:5–6–7) declares that "the mystery of God" shall be finished "in the days of the voice of the seventh angel," according to the good news declared to God's servants, the prophets. The expression, "in the *days,*" signifies a period of time, which may be a number of years. Many events may happen in those "days." But the great event, which awakens the liveliest interest in heaven, is mentioned in the next chapter, in these words: "And the seventh angel sounded (the trumpet); and there were great voices in heaven, saying, The kingdoms of this world are become the Kingdoms of our Lord and of His Christ; and He shall reign forever and ever" (Rev. 11:15).

Thus the *completion* of the "mystery of God" carries us beyond the resurrection and rapture of the saints, into the time when all the world will be under the government of the Lord Jesus Christ.

Also in chapter 12:10 we read (still in the days of the seventh trumpet): "And I heard a loud voice in heaven saying, Now is come salvation and strength, and the *Kingdom of our God*, and *the power of His Christ.*"

That is the event toward which all prophecy points, for which all God's present work is preparing, and for which all creation waits.

Before taking leave of this part of the subject, we would direct special attention to the fact that the distinguishing feature of the Kingdom of heaven is *grace*. God is not now judging any man: "For God sent not His Son into the world to condemn (judge) the world, but that THE WORLD through Him might be saved" (John 3:17). God is not now calling sinners to account, is not imputing their trespasses to them. In one word, He is acting in *grace*, which is just the reverse of *judgment*. In fact, it is stated by the Apostle Paul that, where sin abounded, grace doth much more abound, in order that "as sin hath reigned unto death, so might *grace reign* through righteousness, unto eternal life, by Jesus Christ our Lord" (Rom. 5:21).

The word "grace," therefore, expresses the character of the Kingdom. In this extraordinary Kingdom, *Grace reigns.* That accounts for the fact that there is no judging nor punishing of offenders; for not the *punishment* of sins, but the *forgiveness of sins is now preached.* There is no resistance to enemies and no retaliation, for God is *reconciling* His enemies to Himself by the death of His Son. There is no enforced obedience to the laws of the Kingdom, for the laws are written in the hearts of the children of the Kingdom, not in statute books.

Men may misconstrue the forbearance of God and presume upon it to reject His call to repentance and to scoff at the idea of a judgment to come. To such Paul addresses this searching question: "And thinkest thou this, O man . . . that thou shalt escape the judgment of God? Or despisest thou the riches of His goodness and forbearance and long-suffering; not knowing that *the goodness of God leadeth thee to repentance?*" (Rom. 2:3, 4). And to the same effect Peter declares that the Lord is not slack concerning His promise to come again, as some mistaken men suppose, "but is *long-suffering* toward us, not willing that any should perish, but that all should *come to repentance.*" And he admonishes us therefore to "account that the *long-suffering* of our God is *salvation;* even as our beloved brother Paul also, according unto the wisdom given unto him, hath written unto you" (2 Pet. 3:9, 15).

Inasmuch, then, as grace, forbearance toward wrong-doers, long-suffering with impenitent men, are what characterize the Kingdom of heaven, we should not wonder that, in the Lord's teaching and in that of His apostles, great prominence is given to the command to "judge not" (Matt. 7:1–5; Rom. 2:1; 14:4, 10–13; 1 Cor. 4:5; James 4:11, 12), and to forgive men their trespasses (Matt. 7:14, 15; 18:21–35; Eph. 4:32, etc.). Many other commands and much teaching are given to those who have, by a new birth, entered into the Kingdom of heaven, which commands and teaching are quite contrary to the laws of ordinary kingdoms of this world. But these all are readily seen to be in perfect keeping with the special character of the Kingdom of heaven, in which Kingdom judgment and compulsion have no place, in which forgiveness is the decree of heaven and heaven's King toward *all men,* and in which *grace reigns* through righteousness unto life eternal, by Jesus Christ our Lord. For how can Christ's servants proclaim forgiveness of sins in His Name, if they themselves do not freely forgive all men? And how can they proclaim the complete discharge, through Christ, of all God's just claims upon delinquent sinners, if they demand their own "rights"? Or how can they preach escape from God's judgment for every one who believes in Christ Jesus, if they call others to account to them? How needful, then, is it for us to know what is the character of this wonderful Kingdom, so that our conduct may be in keeping with it. Its one supreme law is *love* (Rom. 13:9, 10). Hence the Word of the Lord to us is this:

> "But I say unto you, Love your enemies, bless them that curse you, do good to them that hate

you, and pray for them which despitefully use you and persecute you; that ye may be the children of your Father which is in heaven. For He maketh His sun to rise on the evil and on the good, and sendeth rain on the just and on the unjust" (Matt. 5:44, 45).

"Be ye therefore followers of God as beloved children" (Eph. 5:1).

We have pointed out the close and intimate connection of Paul's ministry with the announcement of the Kingdom uttered by the Lord Jesus Christ, and with the Lord's revelations of previously hidden truths or "mysteries," which revelations are given in the parables of the Kingdom; and we have been the more impelled to do this because, in certain dispensational views that are popular in these days, the ministry of Paul and that of the Lord Jesus Christ are put far apart, and that of Paul is presented as being of even greater importance than that of his Master.

It would also be profitable to point out (as in the case of the two Scriptures last quoted) the correspondence between the *doctrine* of Paul and that of the Lord, especially as given in the "Sermon on the Mount." We can, however, do no more than to indicate the existence of this correspondence, in the hope that our readers may be prompted to trace it out for themselves.

X

THE MUSTARD SEED AND THE TREE

THE parable of the tares gives a complete outline of the Kingdom of heaven, showing its breadth and length, and showing also its distinguishing characteristics. But there are yet other features or "mysteries" which are revealed by the other parables. Two, the mustard seed and the leaven, are in the same group of three with the parable of the tares, all these having been spoken outside the house in the ears of the multitude. The prominent feature of these three outside parables is *the permitted presence and unchecked working of evil* in the precincts of the Kingdom.

It is sometimes taught that mere "professors," *i. e.*, unconverted persons, churchgoers who make a formal profession of Christianity, are "in the Kingdom." But that view cannot stand in the face of the Lord's positive declarations: "Except your righteousness shall exceed the righteousness of the Scribes and Pharisees, ye shall in *no case enter into the Kingdom of heaven*" (Matt. 5:20). This clearly declares the need of *God's* righteousness, as a condition of entering the Kingdom. To the same effect is Matthew 18:3: "Verily I say unto you, Except ye be converted, and become as little children, ye shall not enter into the Kingdom of heaven"; and John 3:5, "Except a man be born of water and the Spirit he cannot enter into the Kingdom of God." The Pharisees, who were the extreme formalists in that day, were those to whom the Lord said: "Ye shut up the Kingdom of heaven against men; for ye neither *go in* yourselves, neither suffer ye them that are entering to go in" (Matt. 23:13). Thus it clearly appears that the Pharisees, who were mere formal professors, were not in the Kingdom.

To the same effect Paul writes that "the mind of the flesh is enmity against God; for it is not subject to the law of God" (that is, to the control of God) "neither indeed can be" (Rom. 8:7).

Nothing is clearer than that admission to the Kingdom of heaven is *solely by believing the Gospel,* and that the law of the Kingdom is *voluntary obedience* to God—obedience "from the heart."

The facts in this regard are that the *good seed* are "the children of the Kingdom," that neither "the children of the Wicked one," nor "mere professors" are in the Kingdom. But the Kingdom is *in the world* ("the field is the world"), and the other classes of persons are also in the world, and are commingled with the children of the Kingdom so that it is not easy to distinguish them. Hence the Kingdom is "like"—that is, it resembles—things which do not at all suggest its real character.

In the parable of the mustard seed there are three features which are also found in the parable of the tares; namely, *the man,* his *field,* and a *seed* sown in it. This correspondence makes the interpretation easy, and shows why there is no explanation given in the Scripture. The man is Christ; the field is the world; the seed represents that which Christ introduced into the world. But, in this parable, we have only a single seed, and the point to which our attention is called by the Lord's words is the *extreme smallness* of the seed—"the least of all seeds." This speaks of the apparent insignificance of what the Lord brought into the world (when viewed from the ordinary standpoint), in comparison with the great political and religious systems founded by men of the world. Those great systems which attain to earthly prominence and grandeur are likened to *trees*.

Of Christ Himself it is recorded that "He was in the world . . . and the world knew Him not" (John 1:10). And of His true Church it is written: "Therefore the world knoweth us not, because it knew Him not" (1 John 3:1). It follows that, normally, there would have sprung up (and in fact it is so, though the *appearances* are far otherwise) a humble, inconspicuous plant, as lowly and as unpretentious as was He Himself. But the surprising fact which this parable reveals is that, instead of a modest plant, there has developed—*apparently from that tiny seed*—an abnormal growth, "the greatest among herbs," becoming a "tree." This is indeed the aspect, similitude, or *likeness* of that vast far-spreading system, known in the world as the "Christian Religion." That system is recognized by the world as one of "the great religions." It is thus classified among the systems *of the world;* and not only so, but is so to speak "the greatest among herbs." Although the world knew Him not, and knows not us, "the sons of God," yet *it knows this great System very well indeed,* and respects it highly.

From the New Testament Scriptures we know what the Church of God was in its uncorrupted state, when the saints were despised and persecuted, and the Apostles were counted as "the filth *of the world,* and as the offscouring of all things." And, from history, we know how that outward character or *likeness* underwent a marvellous transformation, beginning in the reign of the Roman emperor Constantine, when "Christianity" was made, by royal decree, the acknowledged state religion. Men were forced, by the power of the state, to become "Christians" and to be baptized; and in order to make these unconverted pagans feel less strange in their new "religion," pagan images, pictures, objects of superstitious veneration, ornate ceremonies, magic rites, a priestly class invested with supposed mysterious spiritual powers, and other accompaniments of idolatrous religions, were introduced, being, in most cases, modified and renamed to suit their new environment, but in substance unchanged, and thus affording the opportunity for idolatrous worship to which the natural heart clings with so much tenacity.

And so, by manifold corruptions, and by the addition of many things utterly foreign and opposed to the truth of God, the great "tree" grew apace, and uplifted itself in pride and pretension, towering skyward above all other religious and political systems, not merely seeking recognition and eminence as a great thing in the world, but arrogantly claiming supreme temporal authority over all peoples and governments. Thus we have an abnormal growth, a monstrosity, a complete transformation. For this "tree," whose roots are struck deep in the soil of this corrupt world, from which it draws its nourishment, and whose top aspires to the place of supreme importance, has no trace whatever of the *heavenly* Kingdom which the Lord Jesus brought into the world; but has decked itself with all the trappings and paraphernalia of *earthly* greatness.

For a *tree* is, in Scripture, the symbol of *earthly dominion,* in the nature of national greatness. (See Ezek. 31:2–18; Dan. 4:1–22). As an illustration of this, we need only to refer to Nebuchadnezzar's dream, in which the extension and majesty of his dominion was represented by a great tree "under which the beasts of the field dwelt, and upon whose branches the fowls of the heaven had their habitation."

In the tree of corrupt Christendom, the trunk, rising upward in arrogant pretension, represents the extraordinary growth of the Church of Rome. But from this trunk have sprung many "branches," great and small, having many offshoots, whose number runs into the hundreds. And all these are recognized in the world as "branches of the Christian Church." The "branches" do not, as a rule, aspire *upward,* not claiming authority *over* the state, but project *horizontally,* being quite satisfied to receive respect and support from the world. And such is the position which the great "tree" occupies in the world's esteem to-day, the true Church of God being less "known" than ever.

But now the parable directs, or rather it *focuses*, our attention upon one single fact in connection with this great "tree" of corrupt and apostate Christendom; namely, the fact that "the birds of the air come and *lodge* in the *branches* thereof."

From the parable of the sower we have learned that the birds of the air represent the agents of the Devil, who are ever alert to catch away the "good seed" from the hearts of men. In Christ's day, when He went about preaching the Gospel of the Kingdom, the birds were already active in catching away the good seed. But there was then no "tree," no great institution towering skyward, with wide-spreading branches where the birds could find posts of advantage for carrying on their work. It is different now. For now the birds "come" without hindrance to the tree, are made welcome there, and even *"lodge"* in the *"branches"* of it. This is a "mystery" indeed. But the very thing which our Lord marvellously foretold, in a few words, stands now before our eyes. There is the great tree, with its many "branches," twigs and offshoots. And every branch affords lodgment, support, and the best possible opportunities to the active and dextrous "birds of the air," the agents of "the Wicked one," who assiduously catch away the seeds of truth, sometimes by denial, sometimes by subterfuge, sometimes by skillfully removing the kernel while leaving the verbal husk of sound doctrine. In that way thousands of Satan's agents are incessantly carrying on the work of snatching away from the hearts of men the truths of Christ's Deity, His death for sinners, His bodily Resurrection, His complete Redemption available to all who believe, His coming Glory, Salvation by grace, the Inspiration of Scripture, the Divine authenticity of the Gospel, the truth of eternal judgment—in fact, every "good seed" which the servants of Christ scatter, by His command, in every part of the field.[1]

Such is Christendom in our day. Hence it behoves all "children of the Kingdom," who have connected themselves with any one of the "branches" of the great tree, to ask themselves, "What am I doing here?"—"Is this the place of *God's* choice for me, or am I here by my own choice?" Any who are led to ask that question in sincerity will hear a word like this: "Be ye not *unequally yoked together with unbelievers:* for what fellowship hath righteousness with unrighteousness? and what communion hath *light* with darkness? . . . Wherefore, come out from among them, and be ye separate, saith the Lord, and touch not the unclean thing: and *I will receive you,* and will be a *Father unto you,* and ye shall be *My sons and daughters,* saith the Lord Almighty" (2 Cor. 6:14–18).

Here is a wonderful and blessed promise to such "children of the Kingdom" as will heed God's call to separation from unbelievers. Many hesitate to take the step, and ask, What will happen? Here is

[1] For a specific modern instance of the fulfillment of this prophetic parable see the writer's pamphlet, "Catching away the Good Seed," published by Our Hope Publishing Company, 456 Fourth Avenue, New York. Price, 10 cents.

God's answer, "*I* will receive you." Do we ask for more?

But, as the end draws near, and judgment is about to fall on great Babylon, the call to "come out" changes from the voice of entreaty and promise to that of urgent *warning*. Beloved children of God, who for *any* reason, or under *any* pretext, remain in association with any of the "branches" of the great tree, I pray you hear the *very last call in Scripture* from God to *His* people:

> "Come out of her, *My* people, that *ye* receive not of *her* plagues. For her sins have reached unto heaven, and God hath remembered her iniquities" (Rev. 18:4, 5).

The case of "righteous Lot," whom God did not forget, even when he was willingly associated with the corruptions of Sodom, is the conspicuous Scriptural illustration of the loss which God's people invite and risk when they forsake the path of separation from the world, which is also the path of safety, blessing and fruitfulness for the children of Abraham. The illustration speaks so pertinently and so powerfully that we need only to call attention to it in closing our remarks upon the parable of the great tree.

XI

THE LEAVEN IN THE MEAL

THE parable of the leaven is the shortest of all. "The Kingdom of heaven is like unto leaven which a woman took and hid in three measures of meal till the whole was leavened."

In this parable is given us the third aspect of the unchecked working of evil in the sphere of the Kingdom of heaven. The prominent thing in this word-picture is the *leaven,* and the figurative meaning of that substance has been clearly explained for us by the Lord Himself. As used by Him, it stands for *evil doctrine.* Thus He bade His disciples to "beware of the leaven of the Pharisees, and of the Sadducees" (Matt. 16:6–12), meaning thereby, as stated in verse 12, "the *doctrine* of the Pharisees and Sadducees." And it plainly appears, from Matthew 15:7–9, that the doctrine of the Pharisees is *hypocrisy,* or that religious formalism which corrupts the *truth and worship of God.* For the Lord, after denouncing the Pharisees as "hypocrites," said, "But in vain do they *worship Me, teaching for doctrines the commandments of men."*

In Mark 7:1–13 we have a fuller account of the Lord's warning against the doctrine (*i. e., teaching*) of the Pharisees, showing how they had made the *Word of God* void by their tradition. In rebuking them He said: "For laying aside the *commandment of God,* ye hold the tradition of men"; and, again, "Full well ye reject the *commandment of God* that ye may keep *your own tradition.*"

In studying these and like passages of Scripture, it is needful to bear in mind that "teaching" or "doctrine," in the Biblical sense of that word, is not merely the imparting of certain views of truth, neither is it the exposition of Scripture, nor yet is it prophesying, but it is the giving of instructions *how to act, how to behave, what to do.* "Sound dectrine" is given with the object of producing, not *orthodox opinions,* but *godly behavior* (see 1 Tim. 1:9, 10, and Titus 2:1–10, where specimens of "sound doctrine" are set forth). And this result is accomplished by teaching—not dispensational theories, for example, but—"*commandments of God.*" Thus, in the Lord's first instruction concerning the Kingdom of heaven, He said: "Whosoever, therefore, shall break one of these least *commandments,* and shall *teach* men so, he shall be called least in the Kingdom of heaven: but whosoever shall *do* and *teach* them, the same shall be called great in the Kingdom of heaven" (Matt. 5:19). To the same effect, in His last charge to His disciples, He mentioned three things they were to do: (1) to disciple all nations (*i. e.,* by preaching the Gospel, whereby believers are born again into the Kingdom); (2) to baptize those who become disciples; and (3) to "*teach* them *to observe all things whatsoever I have commanded you*" (Matt. 28:19, 20).

By these clear words we can readily distinguish

teaching from mere exposition of Scripture, or setting forth of views about prophecy, the dispensations, etc., etc. Those things are, of course, useful; but they are not what is commonly meant by the word "doctrine" (or "teaching").

Let it, then, be carefully noted that what is revealed in the parable of the leaven is that sort of corruption which results from doing away with *the commandments of God,* and substituting other rules of conduct. Leaven, itself, is a piece of dough in a state of *decomposition,* caused by the presence in it of tiny organisms, which produce rapid corruption. During this process of corruption a gas is evolved. Hence, when a small piece of leaven, or yeast, is put into a mass of dough, and exposed to gentle heat, two actions occur: (1) the decomposition spreads in every direction throughout the dough; and (2) the gases produced by this fermentation distend the dough, causing it to swell up to an unnatural size and shape.

The action of the woman *hiding* the leaven in the meal, or flour, suggests the stealthy introduction of a foreign substance which, after it has once been introduced, *acts of itself* to influence the mass in which it is embedded. And such is the nature of false teaching which corrupts the *behavior* of the saints. It tends to *spread,* and to produce a "manner of life" displeasing to the Lord. On the other hand, "*sound* doctrine" is that which is "according to godliness" (1 Tim. 6:1-3). The "grace of God" *teaches* us, not so much what opinions we should hold, but how we should *live* in this present age (Tit.

2:11,12). Hence Paul writes to Timothy: "But thou hast fully known my *doctrine, manner of life,*" etc. (2 Tim. 3:10). And he sent to the Corinthian saints Timothy "who," he said, "shall bring you into remembrance of my *ways* which be in Christ, as I *teach* everywhere in *every church*" (1 Cor. 4:17). Thus Timothy was sent to "teach" the right "ways" of the Lord, rather than to impart orthodox views. And it is instructive to note that Paul says this in direct connection with the subject of "the Kingdom of God," and of his own apostolic authority therein, saying in regard to those who were opposing him: "But I will come to you shortly, if the Lord will, and will know, not the speech of them which are puffed up, but the power. For the *Kingdom of God* is not in word, but in power" (verses 19, 20).

It should be noted, too, that "teaching" is entrusted to *men only,* it being strictly forbidden to women. "I suffer not a woman to *teach,* nor to usurp *authority* over the man" (1 Tim. 2:12). For teaching, that is, directing others as to their *behavior,* involves the exercise of "authority"; whereas woman's place is to be not in authority but in "subjection." Nevertheless, although it is forbidden to women to teach, it is not forbidden them to prophesy (except in the assembly) under proper conditions (1 Cor. 11:5; cf. 14:34, 35, noting in the latter the reiterated words, "in the churches," "in the church").

One conclusion that follows from what has been set forth above is that to be "sound in doctrine," and to be "godly in walk" mean virtually the same thing. When John wrote, "If there come any unto you not having *this doctrine,*" he meant not merely a person who held *unorthodox views,* but one who "transgresseth" and is guilty of "evil *deeds*" (2 John 9–11).

Many more Scriptures might be cited to throw light on the subject of "teaching"; but the foregoing will amply suffice to make it quite plain that the action of a *woman* (one who is forbidden to teach) introducing *leaven* (*i. e.,* bad teaching) into the meal, represents a forbidden *action,* introducing an *evil thing.* And in this connection the Lord's reproof of Thyatira is very pertinent: "But I have against thee that thou sufferest *the woman,* Jezebel, who calls herself a prophetess, to *teach* and to mislead my bond-servants to commit fornication, and to eat things sacrificed to idols" (Rev. 2: 20, lit., trans.). Here we have again, in a figure of speech, a *woman* doing the forbidden thing, *teaching,* with the result that Christ's servants are corrupted as to their *conduct.*

Having thus ascertained the figurative meanings of the *leaven,* and the *woman,* we have only to inquire the significance of the "three measures of meal."

Meal, or flour, is the product of that "increase" which God gives by His blessing upon man's planting and watering, which increase is for the sustenance of man's life. Hence, in acknowledgment of God as the Giver of the "increase of the fields," the Israelites were instructed, as an important part of their *worship,* to present an offering of "fine flour." This is called, in the Authorized Version, the "meat offering" (*i. e., food* offering), but more appropriately, in the American Revised Version, the "*meal* offering" (Lev. 2:1–11).

Now, it is directly to our purpose to note the following prohibition: "*No meat offering,* which ye shall bring unto the Lord, shall be *made with leaven*" (verse 11). It is not necessary to inquire into the reasons for this prohibition in the Levitical law, it being enough for our purpose to observe that the parable represents a woman as introducing into the meal offering a substance which the law strictly forbids *and which renders the offering unacceptable to God.*

Referring also to Genesis 18:6, we find the *self-same expression* used by the Lord in the parable, to wit: "three measures of meal;" and since the number "three" is entirely arbitrary (for it might have been two, or six, or any other number), it is quite clear that we have here a designed connection with the offering of "fine meal" which Abraham, through whom all the nations (Gentiles) were to be blessed, commanded Sarah (the *submissive* wife, according to 1 Pet. 3:6) to prepare as an offering to the Lord.

Finally, we would note, as regards the offering of fine meal, that it was to be *anointed with oil,* which is a well-known type of the Holy Spirit.

Having equipped ourselves with these pertinent facts from the Old Testament Scriptures, and bearing in mind that it is to the ministry of Paul that we are specially to look for the carrying out of the Lord's long-hidden (but now revealed) purpose in regard to the *Gentiles,* we will refer briefly to some of Paul's writings.

In Romans 15:15, 16, Paul writes to a Gentile church in these words: "As putting you in mind, because of the grace that is given to me of God, that I should be the minister of Jesus Christ to the Gentiles, ministering *the Gospel of God,* that *the offering up of the Gentiles* might be acceptable, being sanctified *by the Holy Ghost."*

What we should here observe carefully is that "the Gospel of God" was ministered by Paul, not only for the individual and personal salvation of men through faith in Jesus Christ, but also for their *obedience,* that is, as the next verses show, "to make the Gentiles *obedient."* To this end we find, all through the writings of Paul (as well as those of the other Apostles, and in the discourses of the Lord Himself) these two things,—*first,* facts concerning the Lord Jesus Christ and His redeeming work for sinners, to be *accepted* by faith; and *second,* commandments of the Lord Jesus Christ to be *obeyed* through faith, or "from the heart."

Again, in 1 Corinthians, we find much reproof of the saints for *bad conduct* of different kinds; and, in that connection, Paul uses the word "leaven," saying: "Know ye not that a *little leaven* leaveneth the whole lump? Purge out therefore the *old leaven,* that ye may be a new lump, as ye are *unleavened.* For even Christ our Passover is sacrificed for us: therefore let us keep the feast, not with the *old leaven,* neither with the *leaven* of malice and wickedness; but with the unleavened bread of sincerity and truth" (1 Cor. 5:6–8). This Scripture brings to mind another pertinent fact; namely, that during the Passover week, which was a season specially set apart for the worship of the Lord, no leavened bread was to be eaten, and no leaven was even allowed to be in the house.

It is manifest, from the context, that the "lump" (or mass of dough) stands in this passage (1 Cor. 5) for the company of saints in church-fellowship. One of their number was living in an unlawful relation with his father's wife, and Paul charges them, *when gathered together,* in the Name of the Lord Jesus Christ and with His power (see Matt. 18:18–20 for the authority of the Church to bind and loose), to turn that wicked person over to Satan, for the destruction of the flesh, that the spirit might be saved in the day of the Lord Jesus. The example and influence of such bad conduct, even by one person, would act like leaven. It would leaven the whole lump. Hence they must purge it out. In other words, Paul commands them to "put away from among yourselves that wicked person" (verse 13).

This corresponds precisely with the teaching given to the Ephesian saints; namely, that they should put off the "*old* man which is corrupt, according to the deceitful lusts"; and put on the new man, which after God is created in *righteousness* and holiness of *truth* (Eph. 4:17–32). The "old leaven" represents the former bad conduct of Gentiles, when they gave themselves over "unto lasciviousness to *work all uncleanness with greediness"* (verse 19). To be "unleavened" is to be characterized by "sincerity and truth"; and with this corresponds the commands:—"Wherefore *putting away* lying, speak every man *truth* with his neighbor. . . . Let him that stole, steal no more, but rather let him labor, working with his hands . . . that he may have to give. . . . Let no corrupt communication proceed out of your mouth, but that which is good to the use of edifying. . . . Let all bitterness, and wrath, and anger, and clamor, and evil-speaking, be *put away* from you, with all *malice:* and be ye kind one to another, tender-hearted, forgiving one another, even as God for Christ's sake hath forgiven you."

This is an excellent specimen of that wholesome and *sound* "doctrine" which Christ has given to the saints through His apostles; and, moreover, it explains to us what is meant by "leaven" and its effects when introduced among saints, and allowed to work.

It is recorded of the first believers that they "continued stedfastly in the Apostle's *doctrine"* (of which the above is a good example). But the parable of the leaven in the meal leads us to look for the prevalence of bad conduct, that is to say, for departures from the commandments of the Lord Jesus Christ, to such an extent as is indicated by the words "till the whole was leavened."

In the fifteenth chapter of 1 Corinthians, the effect of tolerated evil is stated in the words: "Evil communications (lit., companionships) *corrupt* good manners. Awake to *righteousness,* and *sin not*" (verses 33, 34). And, in Galatians 5:9, Paul again uses the expression: "A little leaven leaveneth the whole lump." He there was reproving the Galatians because, under the influence of *wrong teaching,* they were *not obeying the truth* (verse 7).

We gather therefore from the parable of the leaven, that bad teaching was to be introduced, in the course of time, into the sphere of the Kingdom, and was to spread throughout the same. In other words, that bad doctrine would appear in the places where the doctrine of Christ had been given (just as tares were to be sown among the wheat), thus producing behavior contrary to the doctrine of Christ, as given in the Sermon on the Mount, and in the latter parts of Romans, Ephesians and Colossians. And this evil was to develop to such an extent as to make the "whole lump" an abomination, and an affront to God. The worship offered by those who thus set aside the "wholesome words, even the *words of our Lord Jesus Christ,* and the *doctrine* which is according to godliness" (1 Tim. 6:3) is vain, and worse than vain; for it is an offense to God. The condition is similar to that which the Lord denounced through Isaiah, saying: "To what purpose is the multitude of your sacrifices unto Me? . . . . Bring no more vain oblations; incense is an abomination unto Me." And the remedy was, "Wash you, make you clean; put away the evil of your *doings* from before Mine eyes; cease *to do* evil; learn to *do* well; seek judgment, relieve the oppressed, judge the fatherless; plead for the widow" (Isa. 1:10–17).

And, again, through another prophet, the Lord refused worship from those who had corrupted their *ways*, saying:

> "I hate, I despise your feast days; and I will not smell in your solemn assemblies. Though ye offer Me burnt offerings and your *meat offerings*, I will not accept them; neither will I regard the peace offerings of your fat beasts. Take thou away from Me the *noise* of thy songs; for I will not hear the melody of your viols" (Amos 5:21, 24).

From this we can get an idea of how the Lord regards the musical renderings and organ accompaniments which form a large part of what is called "worship" in our day, and in which many take part who give no heed at all to "the doctrine of Christ," but indulge in every manner of wickedness, worldliness, and self-pleasing. And what the Lord demanded in lieu of such offensive "worship" was declared in these words: "But let judgment run down as waters, and righteousness as a mighty stream" (Amos 5:21–24).

The three parables which we have now reviewed foretell the mystery of the working of evil, unchecked by Divine power, in the sphere of the Kingdom of heaven, each parable giving one of the special forms in which the working of evil proceeds during "this present *evil* age" (Gal. 1:4).

According to the first parable, there were to be various systems of deadly error springing up in the places where the "good seed" of the Gospel should be sown.

In the second parable we see in prophetic symbol the great and wide-spreading "tree" of apostate Christendom, with its many "branches" affording security and support to the numerous agents of the wicked one who devote their energies to snatching away the words of truth and life.

In the third parable we see the corruption of *doctrine* spreading throughout the "lump" that represents Christianity in the sight of men, resulting in departures from Christlike conduct.

All these things are now in evidence before our eyes. The prophecies contained in the Lord's wonderful word-pictures have come to pass. The end of all things is at hand. Let us therefore watch and be sober.

But this is only one side—the outside—of the picture of the present age which the Lord has given us in His wonderful parables of the Kingdom. And it is the dark side of the picture, that which *appears* on the surface of things. There is another, and a brighter side, which can be viewed by those to whom "it is given to know the mysteries of the Kingdom of heaven." To that other side we now turn our eyes.

XII

THE INSIDE VIEW OF THE KINGDOM

WE have seen that the three parables spoken by the Lord outside the house, in the hearing of the multitude, present an "outside" view of the likeness of the Kingdom during this age while the King is "invisible" in the heavens. Had the Lord left the matter there, the prospects of His disciples for the age then beginning would have been gloomy and discouraging. The prominent thing before their minds would have been the prevalence and development of evil in all parts of the world to which the Kingdom was to extend. But the three parables He spoke to His disciples privately, after coming *inside* the house, give a very different view of the subject.

The first incident, after the Lord sent the multitudes away and entered the house, was a request from the disciples that He would explain to them "the parable of the tares of the field." In response He gave them, in words that are marvellously clear and concise, an explanation of every feature of that parable. Let us remember, then, that our gracious Lord is just as accessible to us (though now He is enthroned in heaven) as He was to them. Hence we can always seek Him to enlighten our ignorance, and to open our understanding that we may understand the Scriptures (Luke 24:45).

The three parables to which we now come have a prominent feature which is common to them all; for each parable tells of something of value that the Lord is securing for Himself out of "this present evil age." Therefore, these parables help to explain the "mystery" of tolerated evil in the world—such, for instance, as the great war of the nations that is just now raging in its fourth year of carnage and devastation. What the Lord is to get out of the world is of so great value as to compensate for all the permitted evils of the age.

Furthermore, the first and second of these parables have another feature in common, namely, that the thing of value which is the subject of the parable (the "treasure" in one case, the "pearl" in the other) is something which the "man" *purchases*, and for which he pays a stupendous price—"all that he had."

The Treasure in the Field

According to a view of this parable which at one time was widely held, the "treasure" was *salvation*, for which a man must give "all he has" (his sinful nature, etc.) in order to secure it. But that view will not bear the test even of a superficial examination. In the first place, it contradicts the fundamental facts of the Gospel, that Salvation is free, that the sinner does not have to "buy" it, and that the sinner has nothing with which he *could* buy it.

Furthermore, the parable speaks not of buying the *treasure,* but of buying the *field.* There is no possible sense in which it could be said that a sinner first finds the treasure of salvation *hidden* in a field, then himself hides the treasure he has found, and then goes and sells all that he has and buys that field.

There can be no doubt at all that, as in the parable of the wheat and tares, the "field" is the world, and the "man" is the Lord Jesus Christ, Who gave His life (thus selling "all that He had") for the redemption of the world. We have, therefore, only to inquire, what does the "treasure" represent?

In Psalm 135:4 we read: "For the Lord hath chosen Jacob unto Himself, and *Israel* for His *peculiar treasure."* At the very beginning, when the Lord made Israel His covenant people, He said: "If ye will obey My voice indeed, and keep My covenant, then ye shall be a *peculiar treasure* unto Me above all people: for all the earth is Mine" (Ex. 19:5). And Psalm 135:4 shows that, although they did not keep His covenant, they nevertheless continue to be, in His unchanging purpose, His "peculiar *treasure."*

To the same effect, Moses said: "For thou art a holy people unto the Lord thy God, and the Lord hath chosen thee to be a *peculiar people* unto Himself above all the nations that are upon the earth" (Deut. 14:2).

The references in these Scriptures to "all people," "all the nations," "all the earth," indicate that the fulfillment of God's purpose for Israel requires that the *whole earth* be redeemed, as well as the *Israelitish nation.* Hence the statement in the parable that the man purchased, not the treasure merely, but the *entire field.* Since Israel is not only to be *saved,* but also is to be placed at the head of the nations of the world, it follows that the fulfillment of prophecy calls for the redemption of the whole world.

The Lord Himself declared that He was not sent but "unto the lost sheep of the house of Israel" (Matt. 15:24); and His statement that He had "come to seek and to save that which was lost" was spoken concerning an Israelite (Luke 19:10). This explains His *finding* the treasure, that is to say, the little "remnant" that "received HIM" (see also Rom. 11:2-5).

The reference to the *hiding* of the treasure is explained by the fact that the nation, Israel, was to be (and has been) *hidden,* so to speak, throughout this age, having no place among the nations of the earth. But God knows where to *find* them.

The words, "and for the joy thereof, goeth and selleth all that he hath," tells of the joy that was set before Him when He endured the cross (Heb. 12:2).

As we have already seen repeatedly, the Apostle Paul is the one who specially takes up the subject of the "mysteries of the Kingdom," and amplifies the Lord's instruction with respect thereto. So, in regard to the parable of the treasure in the field, it is through Paul's ministry that we learn definitely that "God hath not cast away His people whom He foreknew"; and that the blindness in part, which has befallen Israel, will last only "until the fullness of the Gentiles be come in." And then *"all Israel shall be saved;* as it is written, There shall come out of Zion the Deliverer, and shall turn away ungodliness from Jacob." For they are still "beloved for the fathers' sake" (Rom. 11:1, 2, 25, 26, 28).

The fact of the nation Israel being completely hidden, *i. e.*, having no national existence at all during the entire age, and yet existing in God's eye, is one of the striking "mysteries" of the Kingdom of heaven. Previously to A. D. 70 the nation existed as such, though under Gentile domination, and occupied its own country. But at that date it disappeared from view.

Another Scripture, which strongly confirms the above, will be cited in connection with the next parable.

The Pearl of Great Price

> "Again the Kingdom of heaven is like unto a merchantman, seeking goodly pearls: who, when he had found one pearl of great price, went and sold all that he had and bought it."

According to the principles of interpretation that have guided us thus far we are bound to regard the merchantman who came "seeking" something he greatly desired, as representing the Lord Jesus Christ, and to regard the selling of all he had as the giving of His life for the redemption of that which He came to seek. And there is little room for question, we think, that the "*one* pearl of great price" is the *one* Church, which He has redeemed with His own blood.

There are two statements by the Apostle Paul

which agree so closely with the statement of the parable as to exhibit clearly a designed correspondence. To the elders of Ephesus Paul spoke of "the Church of God which He hath *purchased* with *His own blood*" (Acts 20:28). And in writing to the Ephesians he said, "Christ loved the Church, and *gave Himself*" (all that He had) "for it" (Eph. 5:25).

Moreover, the significant word "one," in the parable, brings to mind the many passages of Scripture which declare the *oneness* of those who form the Church, the "*one body,*" the "unity of the Spirit." Particularly it recalls the prayer of the Lord "that they may be *one*" (John 17:21, 22).

Among precious stones the pearl is remarkable in that it is the only one that is produced by *living processes.* A pearl is built up imperceptibly, by forces which work very gradually, and in an *unseen way,* slowly bringing the gem to its complete size and form. The pearl is distinguished, also, for its aspect of unblemished purity and unequalled beauty. Finally, the pearl is unique among gems in that it comes *out of the sea,* which in Scripture stands for the nations of the world (Rev. 17:15). It is out of the sea of nations that the Church is being formed, unnoticed by the eye of the world, being destined for Christ's own possession and adornment, and which Church, in the coming day, He will present to Himself "a Church of *glory,* not having spot, or wrinkle, or any such thing; but . . . holy and without blemish" (Eph. 5:27, 28).

The words of the Apostle James are in accord with

this, when, in stating what the Lord's purpose is for this age, he said: "Simeon (*i. e.*, Simon Peter) hath declared how God at the first did visit the Gentiles to *take out of them a people for His Name.* And to this agree the words of the prophets, as it is written, AFTER THIS I will return, and will build again the tabernacle of David which is fallen down" (Acts 15:47–53).

In John 11:47–53 we find strong confirmation of the explanation that we have given of these two parables. The chief priests and the Pharisees had gathered a council to decide what they should do with Jesus Christ; for they said:

> "If we let Him alone all men will believe on Him, and the Romans shall come and take away both our place and nation. And one of them, Caiaphas, being the high priest that same year, said unto them: Ye know nothing at all, nor consider that it is expedient for us that one man should *die for the people* (Israel), and that the whole nation perish not."

Caiaphas, in speaking those words, was uttering a prophecy without being aware of it; and that prophecy is in agreement with the parable of the treasure. But the inspired Apostle John adds for our benefit the following valuable information:

> "And this spake he, not of himself, but being high priest that year, he prophesied that Jesus should die for that nation; and not for that nation only but that also He should gather together in ONE the children of God that are scattered abroad."

So that we find in this passage of Scripture not only the main features of the explanation we have given of the parables of the treasure and of the pearl, but we find also the words "in *one*," which recall in so marked a way the parable of the "one pearl of great price."

In the order in which the two parables occur, we note the divine order of the Gospel, which is "to the Jew first."

The Drag-Net

In view of what we have found to be the meaning of the two preceding parables, we should expect that the third of the group would also exhibit a company of people saved as the result of the redemption of Christ. This expectation is fully realized, as will now be seen.

The parable of the net bears a certain resemblance to that of the tares, in that it speaks of a separation of the good from the bad. If there were not more in it than that, it would be but a repetition of the other. But there is much more. The Lord gave an explanation of the parable of the net cast into the sea (verses 49, 50), saying: "So shall it be *at the end of the world*"; or, as given in Young's literal translation: "So shall it be at the *full end* of the age." Thus we conclude that the parable points to some event that will take place during the last days of this age.

By the Lord's own prophecy, found in Matthew 24, we learn that during the closing period, called the "end" (or "consummation") of the age, there shall be "*great tribulation,* such as was not since the beginning of the world, no, nor ever shall be"; and that "*immediately after the tribulation of those days* . . . shall appear the sign of the Son of man in heaven . . . and they shall see the Son of man coming in the clouds of heaven with power and great glory" (Matt. 24: 21, 29, 30).

Again, in Revelation 7: 9–17, mention is made of the "great tribulation"(literally, "the tribulation, the great one"), and here we are given a view of an innumerable company gathered out of "*all* nations and kindreds and people and tongues," standing before the throne and before the Lamb. And one of the elders declared that "These are they which came out of (the) *great tribulation,* and have washed their robes and made them white in the blood of the Lamb" (verse 14). It is a redeemed company, gathered out of the "sea" of the nations during the period of the great tribulation. In verses 16, 17 is a reference to the sufferings through which they had passed.

To this final period of turmoil and upheaval of all nations the Lord referred in Luke 21: 25, saying that there should be "upon the earth *distress of nations* with perplexity, the *sea* and the *waves* roaring." But, according to the parable, God will at that time cast a net, as it were, into the raging sea of the nations, and will draw it to the shore "full." That net gathers "of every kind," which corresponds with the fact stated in Matthew 24: 22 that some men ("flesh") will be "saved," that is to say, they will come through that fearful period alive, and be "saved" in that sense. But there will be afterward a separation among those who are to be brought to the shore during the stormy period of the great tribulation. The angels will sever the wicked from the just, and cast them into a furnace of fire.

Thus, the last group of three parables foretells (and other Scriptures confirm the prophecy) that, as the fruit of Christ's redemption, and through God's working in this age, there will be *three* distinct companies of saved people: First, the *nation Israel,* now *hidden* from view nationally, as it has been throughout the age; second, the *Church,* the one pearl of great price; and third,—after the Church has been taken to the glory of the Lord's presence, to be forever with Him (1 Thess. 4:17)—the *Tribulation Saints* (the "good" fish of the parable), an innumerable multitude saved out of all the nations of the earth.

In this connection we would note the present-day miracle of the revival of *national self-consciousness* among the Israelites, which is one of the most wonderful events of these days. And, which is equally marvellous, this newly revived spirit of "Zionism" has received friendly recognition by those great Powers which soon will be able to control the political destinies of Israel, and, along with these stupendous miracles, we see also Palestine and Jerusalem delivered at last from the Turk, and in the hands of a nation most friendly to Israel. These facts testify clearly that "the times of the Gentiles" are very near their end.

XIII

OTHER PARABLES OF THE KINGDOM OF HEAVEN

OUR study of the foreview which the Lord gave of the Kingdom of heaven would be incomplete without at least a brief reference to four other parables found in the Gospel of Matthew. Since it is our purpose to give merely an outline of the subject, and not an exhaustive study of its details, we shall dwell but briefly upon the remaining four of the ten parables of the Kingdom.

The Unforgiving Servant
(*Matt. 18: 23–25*)

This parable is exceedingly important. It teaches, and in a most impressive way, the essential character of the Kingdom of heaven, which character, expressed in one word, is *Grace*. In this wonderful Kingdom there is to be no retribution, no bringing of offenders to judgment and punishment, no calling to account of those who trespass against us; but, on the contrary, the Kingdom of heaven is to be characterized by the full and free forgiveness of all trespasses. For in this Kingdom *grace reigns* through righteousness unto eternal life by Jesus Christ, our Lord (Rom. 5:21).

The very foundations of the Kingdom of heaven are laid in the preaching of repentance and *the forgiveness of sins* in the Name of Jesus Christ (Luke 24:47, and compare Acts 20, verse 21 with verse 25). Every one who enters the Kingdom enters it as a *forgiven sinner,* to whom his Lord has forgiven a crushing debt. That debt, which his Lord has assumed and discharged by giving His own life-blood in payment, is, in comparison to any debt that one believer may owe another, as "*ten thousand talents,*" compared to a "hundred pence." Therefore, if one who has received God's forgiveness of "all that debt" should refuse to forgive a fellow-believer some "debt" due to him (which must in any case be relatively trifling) he would deny the very essence of the Kingdom of heaven, and violate its fundamental principle.

This is what the Lord teaches, in a most solemn and impressive way, by likening the Kingdom of heaven to the case of a servant whose lord had forgiven him a huge debt, "ten thousand talents," and who thereafter "went out and found one of his fellow servants, which owed him an hundred pence," and laid hands on him, demanding instant payment, and refusing even to have patience and to give opportunity for payment to be made. When, in the parable, the matter was brought to the king's notice, he called that servant and said to him: "O thou wicked servant, *I forgave thee* all that debt, because thou desiredst me. Shouldest not *thou also* have had compassion on thy fellow-servant, even as I had pity on thee?" And therefore he delivered him to the tormentors till he should pay all that was due unto him.

The meaning of this parable is given by the Lord Jesus Christ in these words: "So likewise shall My heavenly Father do also unto you, if ye from your hearts *forgive not* every one his brother .their trespasses."

It is clear beyond all doubt that the lesson of this parable is for those whose sins have been forgiven. For it should be carefully noted that the basis of the command that we forgive one another is *God's having first forgiven all that we owed Him—"all* that debt." For we, through the shedding of the blood of Jesus Christ, have been "justified from *all* things" (Acts 13:39); and in Christ "we have redemption through His blood, *the forgiveness of sins"* (Eph. 1:7). We see, then, that the teaching of Paul in his Epistles corresponds exactly, on this fundamental point, with the teaching of the Lord Jesus Christ. For Paul, after telling the Ephesian saints that God had forgiven all their sins, says: "And be ye kind one to another, tender-hearted, *forgiving one another,* even *as God for Christ's sake hath forgiven you.* Be ye therefore followers (or imitators) of God as beloved children" (Eph. 4:32; 5:1 R. V.). Such are the commandments given to "the children of the Kingdom."

This parable also coincides with, and supplements, the Lord's teaching in the "Sermon on the Mount," which contains His commandments for His people in this age. In giving them an example of "the manner" in which they should pray, He taught them to say "and forgive us our debts as we forgive our debtors" (Matt. 6:12). And He draws special attention to this clause, adding: "For if ye forgive men their trespasses, your heavenly Father will also forgive you; but if ye forgive not men their trespasses, neither will your Father forgive your trespasses."

Some expositors have thought that they saw a radical difference between these words of the Lord, and those of Paul in Ephesians 4:32, quoted above; and they have used that supposed difference to sustain the conclusion (most erroneous, in fact, and disastrous in its consequences) that the Lord's words and commandments, as recorded in Matthew, are *not for believers in this age.* Those who hold the above view consistently seek also to divert the Lord's people from *all* His words in *all* the Gospels—for the *same* words of command are found in them all. And the error referred to has logically led some to the extreme view that what is written in Acts, Peter, James, Jude, and the earlier Epistles of Paul, belongs not to this present dispensation, but to some other, either past or future. As opposed to such erroneous and harmful theories the simple truth is that *all* the New Testament Scriptures were written by inspiration of God *after Pentecost,* and for the instruction of His people in this age.

In regard to the specific subject of forgiving others, we have shown (and it is as plain as daylight) that Paul's teaching in Ephesians is precisely the same as the Lord's teaching in the parable of the unforgiving servant. And as regards the prayer in Matthew 6, and the Lord's comment thereon, it is only needful to point out that the subject there is our "trespasses" committed *after* we have been born again and have received the forgiveness of our sins for Christ's sake. Moreover, the form in which the prayer is cast does not fix the measure of God's forgiveness of our trespasses, but it causes us to search our own hearts for any unforgiving thought against another. No child of God should go to his Father asking forgiveness of his trespasses so long as he is refusing forgiveness of his brother's trespasses against himself.

A further lesson, and one of great importance, is to be found in what immediately precedes and gave rise to the parable of the unforgiving servant.

The chapter begins with lessons concerning the Kingdom of heaven, which the Lord illustrates by calling a little child and setting him in the midst of them. Those lessons are, first, that in order to enter the Kingdom one must be converted and become as a little child, this being equivalent to the statement that one must be "born again"; and, second, that those who humble themselves as a little child are greatest in the Kingdom of heaven. Then the Lord, after speaking (verses 7–14) of His jealous care for His "little ones," takes up, at verse 15, the subject of trespasses committed by one brother against another. He gives the rule for dealing with such offenses, saying that the offended one is to go, first, to his brother and tell him his fault *alone*. If he refuse to hear, then the other is to take with him one or two more as witnesses. If he neglect to hear them, the next step is to "tell it to *the Church.*" This leads to a statement of great importance, touching the authority of the Church to bind and loose, and touching the power of the Church ("two or three gathered together *in My Name*") when uniting in prayer. The manner of exercising this authority to bind and loose is shown by Paul's instructions to the Church at Corinth, in regard to "that wicked person." In 1 Corinthians 5:3–5, we read:

> "For I verily, as absent in body, but present in spirit, have judged concerning him that hath so done this deed, *in the Name of our Lord Jesus Christ,* when ye are *gathered together,* and my spirit" (for he was "present in spirit") "to deliver such an one unto Satan for the destruction of the flesh, that the spirit may be saved in the day of the Lord Jesus."

The authority which the Lord thus lodged in the Church, and which was exercised in the instance just cited, has never been withdrawn. Hence it is still to be exercised, in faith and obedience, whenever it becomes necessary to "judge them that are within" (verse 12).

Returning to Matthew 18:21, the next incident is Peter's question: "Lord, how oft shall my brother sin against me, and I forgive him? till seven times?"—and the Lord's reply: "I say not unto thee, Until seven times: but, Until seventy times seven." This leads directly to the parable.

Thus we find here, as in the sixteenth chapter, that the Church of Christ and the Kingdom of heaven are directly linked together, both being definitely located in this age. The authority to judge between brethren ("them which are within") is lodged in the Church; whereas forgiveness of personal grievances, without limit, is the duty of all "the children of the Kingdom."

The Parable of the Laborers in the Vineyard
(*Matt. 20: 1–16*)

This parable does not call for extended comment. From its context it evidently was given to emphasize the contrast between the Kingdom of heaven, and the Kingdom of the Son of man. "In the regeneration, when *the Son of man* shall sit on the throne of *His glory,*" then they who have forsaken all and followed Him, shall occupy stations of honor and dignity (chap. 19:27–30). "But many that are first" (now) "shall be last" (then). This statement, which immediately precedes the parable, is repeated at the end thereof, with the added words: "for many be called, but few chosen" (chap. 20:16). So there can be no doubt as to the point of the lesson. In the Kingdom of heaven, that is to say, in the present era, in which the Lord took the lowly place and was despised, rejected and crucified (verses 17–29), there are to be no posts of honor and dignity. No precedence is to be given to those who bear the burden and heat of the day over those who accept service in the vineyard at the eleventh hour. All fare exactly alike. This equality among all "the children of the Kingdom," the absence of all ranks and distinctions, is only for this age. It is one of the distinguishing features of the Kingdom of *heaven.* In the age to come it will be very different. All the pertinent Scriptures teach the same lesson. See for example verses 25–28 of this chapter (chap. 20) and chap. 23: 8–12.

The words, "many are called but few chosen," we take to mean that many hear the call of the Gospel, accepting God's offer of salvation; but few are chosen for the honors of the coming day of Glory (see Matt. 22: 14).

The Marriage Supper
(*Matt 22: 1–14*)

This parable gains in clearness, and in the point of its application, by contrast with the parable of the Vineyard in the latter part of the preceding chapter. The parable of the Vineyard is not a parable of the Kingdom of heaven; and the significance of this will be evident when we note that it has to do wholly with the treatment which Israel accorded to the prophets whom God had sent unto them; and that it culminates with the sending of the "Son," whom they caught, cast out of the vineyard and slew. In Scripture the Lord's Vineyard represents Israel (Isa. 5: 7). So this parable historically occurs *before* the era of the Kingdom of heaven, and extends to the beginning thereof. Hence it is very significant that the Lord directly joined to the parable of the Vineyard, that of the Wedding Supper, introducing the latter with the now familiar words: "The Kingdom of heaven is like unto . . ."

This parable is very easy to understand, and it fixes beyond doubt the historical position of the

Kingdom of heaven, showing that it unquestionably belongs to this age. The invitation to the wedding, which the King sent forth by his servants, has always been understood as representing the Gospel, and the supper as representing the blessings whereof sinners are invited by the Gospel to partake; which interpretation is indubitably correct. Those who were bidden, to whom the first "call" was sent, and who "would not come," were the unbelieving Jews (comp. John 5:39, 40). Some of them "made light of it," and others maltreated the King's servants, even killing some of them. For this cause "he sent forth his armies, and destroyed those murderers, and burned up their city." Beyond all question, this is a prophecy of the destruction of Jerusalem, which was accomplished by the Roman armies under Titus, in A. D. 70.

Inasmuch as those who were first bidden (the Jews) were not worthy (verses 8–10), the "King" sent his servants *out* into the highways, telling them to gather as many as they should find. This assuredly foretells the sending of the Gospel out among the Gentiles.

As a specific fulfillment of this parable, we refer to the experience of Paul and Barnabas in Antioch of Pisidia (Acts 13). After they had preached Christ in the Jewish synagogue, declaring that unto them the word of this salvation had been "sent" (verse 26); and after the Jews had spoken against these things, contradicting and blaspheming, "*then* Paul and Barnabas waxed bold, and said, It was *necessary* that the *Word of God* should *first* have been spoken to you: but seeing ye *put it from you,* and judge yourselves *unworthy* of everlasting life, lo, we turn to *the Gentiles.* For so hath the Lord *commanded us*" (Acts 13:45, 46).

See also Acts 28:17–31, where we read how Paul first "called the chief of the Jews together," and to them "expounded and testified the *Kingdom of God,* persuading them concerning Jesus, both out of the law of Moses and out of the prophets, from morning till evening"; after which Paul applied to them the same words of Isaiah which the Lord had applied to the Palestinian Jews (as recorded in Matt. 13), adding the words: "Be it known, therefore, unto you, that the *salvation of God* is sent unto the Gentiles, and that they will hear it." And it is recorded that, after this, "Paul dwelt two whole years in his hired house, and received all that came unto him, *preaching the Kingdom of God,* and teaching those things which concern the Lord Jesus Christ."

These Scriptures furnish additional links between the ministry of the Lord Jesus and that of Paul; they furnish incontrovertible proof that the Kingdom of heaven is in this present age; and they show that "preaching the Kingdom of God" is one and the same thing with preaching "the salvation of God," or in other words, "preaching the Gospel."

The incident of the man who was found without the wedding garment shows the necessity of being clothed with *God's* righteousness in order to enter the Kingdom of heaven. (See Matt. 5:20; Rom. 3:22, 23.)

The Parable of the Virgins
(*Matt. 25:1-13*)

This parable foretells what the Kingdom of heaven will be like at the end of the age, and was given to teach to the Lord's people the importance to them of *watching* and *being ready*. Much time and space would be required for the discussion of this parable: so, instead of a comment upon it, we refer the reader to our pamphlet, "Watch, Be Ready."[1]

This parable and that of the "talents," which joins it so closely as to form part of it, teach very strongly that there will be rich rewards for those saints who are "faithful" even "over a few things," and correspondingly bitter disappointments for those who are neglectful, slothful, and disobedient.

Incidentally, we would point out that there is manifestly a vast difference between the place of "weeping and gnashing of teeth" (which speaks merely of sore disappointment—Matt. 24:51; 25:30), and the place of "everlasting fire, prepared for the devil and his angels" (Matt. 28:41).

[1] Gospel Publishing House, 692 Eighth Avenue, New York City, N. Y. Price 10c.

XIV

THE CHURCH AND THE KINGDOM

WE have sought, in the preceding pages, to bring clearly before our readers the leading facts revealed in the Scriptures concerning the Kingdom of heaven, which is the subject announced at the very beginning of the New Testament, being proclaimed by the Lord Jesus Christ Himself. That Kingdom is, no doubt, the prominent subject of the New Testament, and it occupies, along with the Church, the place of central importance in this present age. There exist in many minds uncertainty and confusion concerning the Kingdom of heaven, resulting from erroneous views, which have been widely accepted, and which displace the Kingdom of heaven from the position which God has given it in His plan of the ages. Such dislocation of God's plan by postponing the Kingdom to another dispensation involves the very serious consequence of separating the Lord's people in this age from His own "words," "sayings," and "commandments," which have been given to them for their protection and guidance, and for the proof of their love toward Himself (John 14:15; 1 John 2:4). Against this serious danger we desire to guard our readers, and hence have made special effort to show that the Kingdom of heaven belongs to this present age, and to none other.

We believe that it is quite plain, in the light of the Scriptures, that the work of God in this age has to do with the *Church of God* and *the Kingdom of heaven.* We have seen that, as regards the former, the Lord said: "On this rock I will build My Church, and the gates of hell shall not prevail against it"; and as regards the latter He said to Peter, "I will give unto thee the keys of the Kingdom of heaven." Having discussed the Church and the Kingdom separately, we wish now to view them together, in order to show how they are related and how distinguished.

The Church, then, is a *building,* a "holy temple," which the Lord Himself is erecting for God's "habitation." Jesus Christ Himself is the "sure Foundation," the "Living Stone" on which that Temple is being erected. All who believe on Him, as the result of hearing the Gospel, being quickened by the Spirit, become "living stones," and are fitted into their place according to the plan of the Builder, "being builded together for an habitation of God through the Spirit" (Eph. 2; 1 Pet. 2). The work is long, occupying the entire age for its completion; but however long, the day of its completion must come at last.

In the work of bringing men out from the Kingdom of Satan into the Kingdom of God, human agents are employed. The doors of that Kingdom were thrown open by Peter, first to Jews and then to Gentiles. And evangelists are still used to preach the Gospel whereby pardon and life come to those who believe on the Lord Jesus Christ and own Him as Lord. Water-baptism in the Name of Christ stands at the threshold of the Kingdom, symbolizing the believer's death to the dominion of sin, and his entrance into the Kingdom of God as one who is "alive from the dead." Those who repent and believe the Gospel are baptized by the Lord Jesus Christ with the Holy Spirit. But now we have the building of the Church of God, as to which it is written that "By one Spirit are we all baptized into one body" (1 Cor. 12:13). This baptism by the Spirit manifestly refers to the building of the Church which is being "builded for an habitation of God *through the Spirit*" (Eph. 2:22). The Greek words here translated "through the Spirit," are the same as in 1 Corinthians 12:13 rendered "baptized *by* the Spirit" into the one body. The Spirit is the Divine Agent in that work.

Thus the Church of Christ—that which He called "My Church"—is typified by the Temple, planned by David, and built by David's son Solomon, without the sound of a hammer or other tool, out of choice stones and timbers fashioned and shaped before being put together. It follows that the Church, in the broad, primary meaning of that word, embraces all saints of God, including (1) the many who have passed away (for the gates of hades, the place of the departed, shall not prevail against the carrying out of this purpose); (2) the relatively few believers now living on earth; and (3) those who yet shall believe in Jesus Christ to the end of the age. When this marvellous Building is at last completed, then the Builder will present it to Himself, which will take place in the age to come.

The Kingdom of heaven is not a house, but is a planting in a *field*, which is now under cultivation, whereof God is the Owner, the Husbandman, Who has redeemed it, and is planting, watering and tending it, with a view to a "harvest" at "the end of the age." The saints of God, who are the "living stones," whereof the House is builded, are likewise "the children of the Kingdom." Manifestly their relations as such are different from their relations as parts of God's "spiritual house."

Viewed from God's side, and as His work, the labor of the Kingdom is regarded as *husbandry* or tillage, whereas the labor bestowed on the Church is likened to the construction of a great building. The difference is stated by Paul in 1 Corinthians 3: 5-11, where he speaks of himself, Apollos, Peter and other servants of the Lord as "laborers together with God." He first speaks of the labor of the field, saying: "I have planted, Apollos watered; but God gave the increase." And in this connection he says to the Corinthian saints: "Ye are God's *husbandry*." Here plainly the Kingdom is in view. But he immediately says to the same saints: "Ye are God's *building*"; and as regarding the labor connected with the Church, he says: "According to the grace of God which is given unto me, as a wise *master-builder*, I have *laid the Foundation*, and another buildeth thereon. (But let every man take heed how he buildeth thereupon.) For other Foundation can no man lay than that is laid, which is Jesus Christ."

This Scripture gives very clearly the two aspects of God's work in this age. God is sowing the seed and cultivating the field with a view to the "increase," this being the Kingdom-aspect of His work; and He is building the house for His eternal habitation, this being the Church-aspect of His work.

The Apostle Peter likewise presents this double aspect of the work of God in this age, and in the same order. First, he refers to the new birth given to believers, whereby they are born again into the Kingdom by means of the incorruptible seed, namely, the Word of the Lord which "endureth forever," this being in contrast to the natural man who like the grass of the field "withereth," and like the flower of grass "falleth away" (1 Pet. 1:23–25). Then immediately he proceeds to speak of the building of God's "spiritual house," and describes believers as "living stones" and as a "holy priesthood"—referring to their position in the *house;* and also as a "chosen generation, a holy nation"—referring to their position in the *field.*

There is a wonderful harmony, manifested in many and important correspondences, between Peter's ministry in his first Epistle, and Paul's ministry in his Epistles to the churches, especially Ephesians. The tracing out of those correspondences will be found, by all who undertake it, an exceedingly interesting and profitable study.

The foregoing will suffice to show how the Church

and the Kingdom differ as viewed from God's side, and when regarded as the work which He is carrying to completion in this age. When viewed from *our* side, it is seen that while we (believers in the Lord Jesus Christ) are both in the Church and in the Kingdom, our relations and responsibilities in the former are somewhat different from our relations and responsibilities in the latter.

As members of Christ's body, the Church, our responsibility is to "build up," that is (using the word ordinarily employed in the A. V.) to "edify." This *edifying* applies both to the Church as a whole, and to individual members thereof; and the subject is clearly put before us in the fourth chapter of Ephesians. For the purpose of accomplishing this great work of edifying the Body of Christ, and of edifying His members individually, we learn that "grace" is given "to *every one of us,*" in measure differing "according to the measure of the *gift* of Christ" (verse 7). Each saint is, therefore, *responsible for the proper use of the grace given to him,* and should see to it that he "receive not the grace of God in vain" (2 Cor. 6:1). For Christ builds His Church by *bestowing gifts upon His saints,* and by their use of those gifts (verses 7–12). Thus there is a sense in which the Church *edifies itself,* being built up "by that which *every joint* supplieth" through the "effectual working in the measure of *every part*" (verse 16).

The *method* by which this great work is carried on is by *love.* All effectual work on that edifice is done in the energy of love. For *"love edifieth," i. e.*, builds up (1 Cor. 8:1). And it is important to note that *love*, in the Bible sense of the word, is not merely a sentimental feeling of fondness and desire, but a *mighty force*, which spends itself in *doing* for others, at one's own cost. The manifestation of "the love of Christ which passeth knowledge" is the giving of *Himself* for the beloved object—the Church, and the individuals who compose it. Love is the law which governs (so to speak) God's own actions, for "God *is* love," and His actions express what He is. Therefore, love is the law of God's Kingdom, and to be perfect in love is to be perfect in all things.

Pursuing this line of truth, as given to us in 1 Corinthians, we find, in chapter 12, a list of the various gifts bestowed upon Christ's members; and the same statement is made as in Ephesians 4:7, namely, that "the manifestation of the Spirit is given to *every man*" (*i. e.*, to each member) "to profit withal," or in other words *to be put to its appropriate use*. The direct agency of the Holy Spirit in building the Church by distributing gifts for that use should be noted. In chapter 13 is found that wonderful passage concerning *love*. Its occurrence between the portion which describes the gifts of Christ to His members, and the portion (chapter 14) which describes the purpose and use of those gifts in the Church, is very significant. Why is it there? Manifestly because, *without love*, which is the *power that builds up*, the possession of all gifts—whether of ability to speak the languages ("tongues") of men or even of angels; or that of prophecy and understanding of all mysteries; or of faith even to remove mountains—would be "nothing." The gifts are bestowed for the one purpose of *edification*, and *love* is the energy or power by which each gift must be exercised. Hence, without love, the gifts would be useless; there would be no building up; the result would be "nothing."

So we have this exhortation: "Follow after love, and desire spiritual gifts, but rather that ye may prophesy" (14:1). Why is prophesying to be preferred? Because "he that prophesieth speaketh unto men to *edification*" (verse 3); and again "he that prophesieth *edifieth the Church*" (verse 4).[1] In verse 5, we are again reminded of God's great purpose, namely, "that the Church may receive *edifying*." And further on we read: "Forasmuch as ye are zealous of spiritual gifts, *seek that ye may excel to the edifying of the Church*" (verse 12). If a person prays in a "tongue" (*i. e.*, a foreign language), the result is "unfruitful"; and likewise if one gives thanks in a "tongue," there is no profit, for "the other is *not edified*" (verses 14–17). Hence, the doctrine as to the use of the gifts is summed up in the general exhortation of verse 26: "Let all things be done *unto edifying*."

In view of this clear and important teaching we would do well to examine ourselves by asking what attention are we giving to the work of *edifying* the

[1] It should be noted that "prophesying," in this chapter, means giving the word or message of God in the broad sense, not the foretelling of events. To prophesy is, primarily, to *speak for* another; in this case *for God*.

body of Christ, and what use are we making of the gifts we have severally received to that end?

The same teaching is given in Ephesians 4, where we read that Christ's gifts have been bestowed for the *work* of the ministry, for "the *edifying* of the body of Christ"; that we are to speak "the truth *in love,*" "making increase of the body unto the *edifying* of itself in *love";* and that we should "let no corrupt communication proceed out of our mouth, but that which is *good* to the use of *edifying*" (verses 12, 15, 16, 29). It is easy to see that all this is the carrying out of the Lord's purpose which He declared in the words: "I will build (edify) My Church." And it is very clear that the chief duty of the members of Christ is to make the fullest use of the gifts bestowed upon them for the building up of one another in the energy of love, "which is the bond of perfectness."

As "children of the Kingdom," our relationships and responsibilities are broader, seeing that they pertain to the "field" instead of to the "house." They include all our duties and obligations to the State, and to the people of the world. Thus, in Romans 12, we find verses 4–13 to contain teaching as to our duties toward one another. This is *church*-teaching, the basis of it being set forth in the statement that "we, being many, are *one body* in Christ, and every one members one of another" (verse 5). And in this connection reference is made to the gifts and their use, prominence being given to the exhortations: "Let *love* be without dissimulation;" "Be kindly affectioned one to another with brotherly *love.*"

Then, from verse 14 of chapter 12 to the end of chapter 13, we find *Kingdom* teaching,—commandments being given for governing our conduct toward our fellow men, including our enemies, and toward the civil governments, "the powers that be."

Thus far, in speaking of "the Church," we have confined ourselves to that meaning of the word which it has in Matthew 16:18, where it first occurs. But the Lord used the word a *second* time, and in a *different* sense. We deem it a matter of great significance that we find only two recorded usages of the word "Church" by the Lord while on earth, and that in those two occurrences we have the two different aspects of that important word. In Matthew 18:15–20 the Lord speaks of "the Church" as the *local gathering of believers,* saying: "Tell it unto *the Church,* and *if he will not hear the Church,* let him be unto thee as an heathen man" (an outsider) "and a publican" (one who is an unfit associate).

A "Church of God," then, is a company of believers who are gathered *to the Name of the Lord Jesus Christ* in any place. Such a company has, according to the Word of the Lord (which does not pass away, nor change), the following characteristics: *First,* it has the authority of heaven to bind on earth; *Second,* it has the power on earth of prevailing intercessory prayer. Those powers it has, however small its numbers, because *the Lord Himself is there* "in the midst of them."

It is instructive to connect 1 Timothy 3:15, 16 with Matthew 18:18–20, noting that, according to the correct reading, "the house of God" is *a* (not *the*) Church of the living God, a pillar and ground (or support) of *the truth.*" From this Scripture we gather that God undertakes to keep *His* churches free from denials of *the Truth.* And verse 16 tells plainly what is "*the* truth," which is maintained or supported by the "churches of God." It is nothing less than that "mystery of godliness," which is, beyond controversy, "great."

The word "Church" is used in this sense in 1 Corinthians 14, to which we have already referred. We there read: "If therefore the whole Church be come together into one place." See also verses 19 and 28. In verse 33 we read: "For God is not the author of confusion, but of peace, as in all the *churches of the saints.*"

The word "Church," used in this sense, is found also in many other passages in the Acts of the Apostles, and in the Epistles of Paul. Also in James 5:14, and 3 John 9, 10, and in Revelation, chapters 2 and 3.

The "churches of God" still exist, and their essential character and powers, as stated above, are unchanged, however much failure there may have been in apprehending their true character and in exercising the powers with which the Lord has clothed them. The "churches of *God*" may be readily distinguished from the churches of *men* by the human *names* given to the latter (which names are essential to their very existence), and by the human *arrangements* which characterize them—such as the one-man ministry, the clerical class distinguished by a special dress, and by titles (which Christ has forbidden to His servants); the humanly-devised rules, rites, ceremonies, etc., etc.

It is due to the Lord Jesus Christ, the Head of the Church, Who has pledged His personal Presence (a "real presence" truly) in the midst of saints gathered to *His* Name, that every one of His members should be visibly associated with other saints who are gathered to the Name of the Lord. All should give heed to the exhortation "Not forsaking the assembling of ourselves together," and should do so the more faithfully as we "see the day approaching" (Heb. 10:25).

We believe that the divinely-given illustrations of a "field" and a "house" will be a guide to those who wish to trace out in greater detail than we have attempted to do, the distinguishing features of the Kingdom and the Church, and also their connection the one with the other. Broadly speaking the believer's Kingdom-relations are outward, extending to all the world; whereas his Church-relations are inward, extending only to those who are of "the household of God."

The fact that Christ Jesus is the "Son of David," to which prominence is given both in Matthew's Gospel and Paul's (Matt. 1:1; Acts 13:22, 23; Rom. 1:3; 2 Tim. 2:8) is another link between the Kingdom and the Church; since it was promised of David's seed that He should both build the House of God and also occupy the throne of God's Kingdom.

XV

THE GLORY

"The Lord will give GRACE *and* GLORY*"*
(Psa. 84:11)

IT is easy to see that the double promise of the verse quoted above covers two great ages in God's eternal plan. The present age is characterized by *grace*. "For the *grace* of God that bringeth Salvation hath appeared unto all men" (Titus 2:11). *"Grace* . . . came by Jesus Christ" (John 1:18). Thus the word "grace" is associated with the first coming of the Lord Jesus Christ. Grace is the chief subject of the ministry of His servant Paul, who counted not his life dear unto himself, so that he might finish his course, and the ministry which he had received of the Lord Jesus, namely, "to testify the Gospel of the *grace* of God" (Acts 20:24). And, as we have seen, grace is the essential characteristic of the Kingdom of heaven; for the throne of that Kingdom is a "throne of grace" (Heb. 4:16).

On the other hand, the word which is most conspicuously employed in Scripture to characterize the coming age is "Glory." The promised gift of "Grace" has been fulfilled through the Lord's first coming in *weakness*. The promise of "Glory" will be fulfilled at and through His second coming in *power*. And as the promised "grace" has far exceeded all that prophets and righteous men of old could have imagined, so the coming *glory* will doubtless exceed immeasurably all that our hearts could desire or our minds conceive. Hence this chapter is written, not with any expectation of explaining what the "glory of the Lord" will be like, but simply with the object of bringing to the reader's attention a few of the many Scriptures that foretell that coming "glory." No doubt those Scriptures will produce a happy effect upon the reader's mind.

In seeking to understand in some measure what is meant by the word "glory," it will help us to remember that that word describes *the state or condition of God's own Being.* Moses desired that he might behold the "glory" of the Lord. But God said: "Thou canst not see My face: for there shall no man see Me and live." And further the Lord said: "It shall come to pass that, while *My Glory* passeth by, I will put thee in a clift of the rock, and will cover thee with My hand while I pass by" (Ex. 33:18–23).

Of the Son of God it is written that He is "the brightness," or effulgence, of the Father's "glory" (Heb. 1:2). It is of this "glory" that the Lord Jesus spoke to His Father in His prayer, recorded in John 17: "And now, O Father, glorify Thou Me with the GLORY which I had with Thee before the world was" (John 17:5).

"Glory" is, moreover, the condition in which the Lord Jesus entered heaven, after His sufferings and humiliation on earth were ended. The Apostle's description of the great mystery of godliness begins with the words: "God was manifest in the *flesh*" (that is, in humiliation), and ends with the words, "received up into (or *in*) *glory*" (1 Tim. 3:16). We have these two parallel expressions "manifested in *flesh*" describing the first appearing ("epiphany") of Christ, and "manifested in *glory*" (Col. 3:4), describing the second epiphany of the Lord, when His redeemed people shall be "manifested with Him."

This "glory" which Christ has as a *Man*, risen from the dead and received up into heaven, is referred to by Him in the prayer already quoted, in which He says: "And the *glory which Thou gavest Me*, I have given them" (John 17:22). The glory which Christ Jesus has received as the Redeemer is that which He purposes to share with His own redeemed people. God's ultimate "purpose" for them whom He has "called" and "justified," is that they be also "*glorified*" (Rom. 8:30). Those who have been "justified freely by His *grace*" and who now have "access by faith into this *grace* wherein we stand" also "rejoice in hope of the *glory* of God" (Rom. 3:24; 5:2). For the work which God is accomplishing in this age, through the High-Priestly work of Christ, is "bringing many sons unto *glory*," in the accomplishing of which work He is "the Captain of their salvation" (Heb. 2:10).

The Apostle Peter, also, who takes up the theme of "the sufferings of Christ and the GLORY that should follow," speaks of the appearing of Jesus Christ "with joy unspeakable and full of *glory*"

(1 Pet. 1:7, 8). Again he says: "But rejoice, inasmuch as ye are partakers of Christ's sufferings, that when His *glory* shall be revealed, ye may be glad also with exceeding joy." He also reminds us that "the God of all *grace*" has "called us unto His eternal *glory* by Jesus Christ" (1 Pet. 4:13; 5:10).

The Lord Jesus Christ Himself has repeatedly referred to that day of "glory," which shall be ushered in by His second coming. In Matthew 16:27, immediately after He had showed to His disciples the sufferings and death He was about to undergo, He referred to His coming again, saying: "For the Son of man shall come in the *glory* of His Father with His angels." Also He gave to His twelve apostles the following promise: "In the regeneration, when the Son of man shall sit in the throne of His *glory*, ye also shall sit upon twelve thrones, judging the twelve tribes of Israel" (Matt. 19:28). And again: "When the Son of man shall come in His *glory*, and all the holy angels with Him, then shall He sit upon the throne of His *glory*" (Matt. 25:31).

When the Lord returns in power and glory He will be accompanied not only by the angels, but also by His redeemed people, according to the promise: "When Christ, Who is our life, shall appear, then shall ye also appear with Him in *glory*" (Col. 3:4). It is manifest that, in order to appear "*with* Him" they must first be raised and transformed (or, if living at the time of His return, they must be changed into His likeness), and *taken to where He is*. And that is precisely what is to happen, according to Scripture.

In 1 Corinthians 15, we are again carried to the harvest-field; but this time it is with a view to revealing facts concerning the resurrection of the dead. Christ Himself Who, as a grain of wheat, was cast into the ground and died (John 12:24), is the "First-fruits" of the harvest. Afterward, "they that are Christ's *at His coming*" are to be gathered from the earth (verses 20–23). And by the answer given to the question, "With what body do they come?" we learn that "it is sown in dishonor, it is raised in GLORY."

Moreover, in the resurrection, each one will have his own proper *glory*. For as "one star differeth from another star in *glory, so* also is the resurrection of the dead." Thus the dead will be raised in glory like the stars of heaven; for "the heavens declare the GLORY of God." And though "we shall not all sleep," yet "we shall *all* be changed, in a moment, in the twinkling of an eye" (verses 51, 52). And then the dead who are "raised in glory," and the living saints who are transformed in a moment into the likeness of Christ, will be caught up to meet Him in the air, thereafter to return "with Him, in GLORY" (1 Thess. 4:17; Col. 3:4).

The transformation of the saints in bodily appearance is very clearly set forth in Philippians 3:20, 21: "For our conversation (or citizenship) is in heaven; from whence also we look for the Saviour, the Lord Jesus Christ, Who shall *change our vile body,* that it may be fashioned *like unto His glorious body,* according to the working whereby He is able even to subdue all things unto Himself." In this passage, the original words are "the body of His *glory*"; which has been rendered "glorious body." Thus the translation hides the fact that the characteristic word "glory" is here used.

In various other passages, to which we will now refer, the word "of glory" in the original text has been rendered by the adjective "glorious"; and while the meaning is practically the same, yet the truth expressed is more forcibly presented by a literal rendering.

Thus, in Titus 2:11, already referred to as declaring that the "*grace* of God that *bringeth salvation* hath appeared," we read, also, that grace teaches us how to live "in this present age" while "looking for that blessed hope and the *glorious appearing* of the great God and our Saviour Jesus Christ." What is here seen to be the prospect toward which we should ever be looking as our "blessed hope," is "the appearing of the GLORY of the great God and our Saviour." And by thus reading the passage, according to the literal rendering, we see an instructive parallel between verse 11 and verse 13. In the former we have the appearing of the *grace* of God, and in the latter the appearing of the *glory* of God. Thus the passage reminds us of the promise: "the Lord will give *grace* and *glory*." The grace we have already received, and the glory we are "looking for."

In 2 Corinthians 4:3, 4, the Apostle Paul speaks of those who are "lost" (*i. e.*, are perishing) "in whom the god of this world (age) has blinded the minds of them which believe not, lest the light of the *glorious Gospel* of Christ, Who is the image of

God, should shine unto them." Again, by reading "the Gospel of *the glory* of Christ" the passage gains in force and clearness. There are those whose minds are blinded so that they cannot receive even a glimpse of the *glory* of the coming day of Christ. The god of *this* age (the devil) has dazzled them with the false and transient glories of this present world, leading them to expect great benefits, gains and improvements through the efforts of man in the line of civilization, scientific discoveries, and the like. Into minds that are thus blinded no gleam of the light of "the Gospel of the GLORY of Christ" has penetrated.

In Romans 8, the hope of the coming GLORY is clearly presented in verses 16–30. The Apostle declares that "the sufferings of this present time are not worthy to be compared with the GLORY which shall be revealed in us." And in this passage is made known the important fact that the groaning creation itself will share in the blessings and deliverance of the coming day, when the sons of God (who now groan within themselves, waiting for the adoption) shall enter into the *glory* that awaits them. In this connection we read that "the creature (or the creation) itself shall be delivered from the bondage of corruption into the *glorious liberty* (the liberty of the GLORY) of the children of God" (verse 21). Here is a wonderful deliverance for creation, from "bondage" into "liberty." Corruption has fastened itself upon the creation of God as a species of bondage. But at the coming of Christ, when the children of God will enter into their "glory," then creation also will be delivered, and will enter into the liberty that will everywhere prevail, in the day of "the *glory* of the children of God." In that day, many Old Testament prophecies will be fulfilled, such as Psalms 96:10–13; 97:1; Isaiah 35:1–10, etc.

In Ephesians we read of those who are saved by *grace* and predestinated to *glory*. These are already quickened together with Christ, being made, by grace alone, the "members of His body, of His flesh and of His bones" (Eph. 5:30). As sharers of His life now, they will share His glory in the approaching day. For "Christ also loved the Church, and gave Himself for it . . . that He might present it to Himself a *glorious* Church (a Church of GLORY) not having spot, or wrinkle, or any such thing; but that it should be holy and without blemish" (Eph. 5:25–27).

"The Church which is His body" is now a thing unknown and unnoticed in the world, though it reveals to the principalities and powers in heavenly places the manifold wisdom of God. But soon it will be "a Church of GLORY," whose dazzling brightness and splendor will be displayed in the eyes of the entire universe. This will surely come to pass; for to this end Christ "gave Himself"; and it is the eternal purpose of Him "Who is able to do exceeding abundantly above all that we ask or think, according to the power that worketh in us. Unto Him be GLORY in the CHURCH by Christ Jesus, unto all the generations of the age of the ages. Amen."

"Then let us, brethren, while on earth,
With foes and strangers mixed,
Be mindful of our heavenly birth,
Our thoughts on GLORY fixed."

Appendix

NOTE ON THE SERMON ON THE MOUNT

Salt and Light

THE New Testament Scriptures were completed by the writings of the Apostle John not far from the year 100 A. D. Those Scriptures, therefore, in their completed form, were given to the Church of God about seventy years after the ascension of the Lord Jesus Christ into heaven. We should bear in mind that the Gospels are not contemporaneous records of the Lord's acts and words—the things He "began both to do and teach, until the day in which He was taken up" (Luke 1:1, 2)—but were written under inspiration of the Holy Spirit *many years afterward.* In them (the Gospels) is fulfilled the Lord's promise when He said (speaking of His own words which those who love Him are to keep):

> "These things have I spoken unto you, being yet present with you."

But how were His words to be guarded against loss through the infirmity of human memory? In this way:

> "But the Comforter, which is the Holy Ghost, Whom the Father will send in My Name, He shall teach you all things, and *bring all things to your remembrance whatsoever I have said unto you*" (John 14:21-26).

Thus, by the ministry of the Holy Spirit, the Lord insured that His disciples should have a faithful record of His words and commandments, to the end that, in keeping them, they might both show their love for Him, and also enjoy the promise of verses 21, 23. He also, in this way, made it possible for the apostles to carry out the last charge He gave them, namely, to teach His people *to observe all things whatsoever He had commanded them* (Matt. 28:20).

In the Scriptures, as thus completed and given to the Church about seventy years after Pentecost, the Gospel of Matthew is given the foremost place; and the great theme of that Gospel is the Kingdom of heaven. How can we understand the prominence given to the theme of the Kingdom of heaven if that Kingdom was "the earth rule of David's Son," and if it had been offered to the Jews, refused by them, and in consequence postponed for several thousand years? It would be difficult, if not impossible, to account for the New Testament Scriptures in the form in which they have been given to the Church of God, if that theory were correct. But that is not all, nor is it the greatest impediment to the acceptance of that theory. Even if it be conceivable that Christ could have offered the earthly Kingdom to the Jews while as yet all the prophecies, types and shadows of Redemption were unfulfilled, and while the world was perishing under the dominion of sin and death, how even then can we account for the fact that the Holy Spirit not only gave prominence to the Kingdom of heaven in the New Testament Scriptures, but said not a word about its being a name for the "*earth* rule of David's Son," or about its having been offered to the Jews *conditionally*, or about its having been postponed to another age?

The facts (1) that the ministry of John the Baptist, which had to do solely with the Kingdom of heaven, is placed in the foreground of all the Gospels, (2) that prominence is given also to the Lord's unqualified proclamation of the Kingdom of heaven as at hand, and (3) that the Sermon on the Mount, which also has to do with that Kingdom, is given a conspicuous place in the first Gospel, lead necessarily to the conclusion that the Kingdom of heaven belongs to this age. And that conclusion is absolutely established by the absence of any word in the New Testament to the effect that the Kingdom announced by John, and by the Lord Jesus Christ, with all that pertains thereto, has been disconnected from this age, and postponed to the age to come.

What the people of God are most concerned to know (and it is a point about which they cannot afford to be mistaken or even uncertain) is whether the commandments spoken by the Son of God, which His Father gave Him to speak, are applicable directly to them, or are intended for the people of a yet future age. We believe there is not the very slightest ground for the idea that the Lord's words and commandments, recorded in the Gospels, are intended for Jews who shall hereafter be in the earthly Kingdom foretold in the Old Testament prophecies, but that they are applicable to the children of God in this present age.

We believe furthermore that the Sermon on the Mount contains internal evidence which proves in the clearest way that it is spoken directly to the children of God, that is to say to believers in the Lord Jesus Christ. Indeed the fact that the Sermon on the Mount contains the Father's commandments to His children, spoken by the Son in His Father's Name, appears in every part of that great utterance.

We do not undertake at this time an exhaustive presentation of the pertinent evidence contained in the Sermon on the Mount; but propose only to call attention to a small portion thereof, namely to the first sixteen verses of Matthew 5, and particularly to the words "Ye are the salt of the earth," "Ye are the light of the world."

In the "Beatitudes" the Lord defines the character of those who compose the Kingdom of heaven. They are poor in spirit, they mourn, they are meek, they hunger and thirst after righteousness, are merciful, pure in heart, peacemakers, are persecuted for righteousness' sake. These descriptions do not at all fit the Israelites in the promised time of their national greatness; nor do the blessings spoken by the Lord correspond with the blessings covenanted to the Israelites in the time of the restored Kingdom. They are in fact so widely different in kind as to prove conclusively that the two sets of promises belong respectively to different eras. Christ says of those to whom the Sermon on the Mount was spoken, that theirs *is* the Kingdom of heaven, that they *shall be* comforted, *shall* inherit the earth, shall be filled, shall obtain mercy, shall see God, shall be called the children of God. These blessings manifestly are more like the spiritual blessings of Ephesians 1:3, wherewith God has blessed *us* in heavenly places in Christ, than the earthly blessings promised to Israel.

The Lord then pronounces a special blessing upon such of His followers as are reviled and persecuted for His sake, saying: "Blessed are ye when men shall revile you and persecute you, and shall say all manner of evil against you falsely for My sake. Rejoice and be exceeding glad, for great is your reward *in heaven;* for so persecuted they the prophets which were before you."

Clearly those words could not apply to a time when Christ shall be on the earthly throne of David ruling the nations with a sceptre of iron, and dashing in pieces like a potter's vessel such as resist His authority. Moreover, the promised reward to those who thus suffer for Christ's sake is "in heaven." Undoubtedly those words were fulfilled in the experience of the Lord's disciples after His departure; and if so, then the words of the Sermon on the Mount belong to this age.

Then comes the passage in which the Lord declares that His disciples are "the salt of the earth," and "the light of the world." There can be no doubt that these statements apply to the children of

God in this age, and not to the Israelites in the coming day of their earthly supremacy; and if so, then the Kingdom of heaven is in this age, and the Sermon on the Mount is for the Lord's people in this age.

In the first place we are bound to observe the force of the fact that the Lord's words state what His present disciples "*are*," not what some future people of Israel *will be*. That fact is of itself well-nigh decisive; for it would be a most unwarrantable assumption that, when the Lord said "*Ye are* the salt of the earth," and "*Ye are* the light of the world," He meant that some other people, some thousands of years thereafter, would be, at that remote time, the salt of the earth and the light of the world. Such assumptions do violence to the Word of God, and tend to weaken one's confidence in it. But even if it were permissible in any case to take such liberties with plain statements of fact from the Lord's lips, it is certainly inconceivable that the above-quoted words should stand where they do in the completed Scriptures, without a hint from the Spirit of God in the context, or anywhere in the New Testament, that they were spoken of a time and a people thousands of years in the future, if the above assumption were correct.

The words "Ye are the salt of the earth" take us back to Leviticus 2:13:

> "And every oblation of thy meat offering shalt thou season with salt; neither shalt thou suffer the salt of the covenant of thy God to be lacking from thy meat offering: with all thine offerings thou shalt offer salt."

Salt has various properties; but the words of the Lord Jesus in Matthew 5:13 show plainly that it is solely the property of "savor," or taste, that is in view here. Salt then is that which makes the products of nature acceptable to God; and so we learn from this saying that the children of God, those who in this age are counted "righteous" in God's eyes, are the salt of the corrupt earth in that their presence stays the judgment that has long been due.

Those disciples were the justified sinners who were the fruit of John the Baptist's ministry. In them was fulfilled the last prophecy of the Old Testament: "Behold I will send you Elijah the prophet before the coming of the great and dreadful day of the Lord; and he shall turn the heart of the fathers to the children, and the heart of the children to their fathers, lest I come and *smite the earth with a curse*" (Mal. 4:5, 6).

The message of the angel Gabriel applies this prophecy to John the Baptist, of whom he said:

> "And many of the children of Israel shall he turn to the Lord their God. And he shall go before Him in the spirit and power of Elias, to turn the hearts of the fathers to the children, and the disobedient *to the wisdom of the just; to make ready a people prepared for the Lord*" (Luke 1:16, 17).

Again it is written of John's ministry:

> "There was a man sent from God whose name was John. The same came for a *witness* to bear witness of the Light, that all men through him *might believe*" (John 1:6, 7).

Again we have Paul's testimony about John:

> "John verily baptized with the baptism of repentance, saying unto the people that *they should believe on Him who should come after him,* that is on Christ Jesus" (Acts 19:4).

It is clear then that the presence in the earth of those who have God's righteousness by faith in Jesus Christ acts as salt to stay the Hand of God from executing judgment thereon for its corruption. The case of Sodom illustrates the point (Gen. 18:23–32).

It is quite certain that the words, "Ye are the light of the world," apply to the children of God in this age of darkness when Christ the "true Light" is absent. It could not apply to any other people in any other age. When Christ comes again in His glory, it will be "the day." But during His absence His people are to let their light so shine before men that they may see their good works and glorify their Father who is in heaven.

To the same effect Paul says:

> "For ye were sometimes darkness, but now are ye light in the Lord: walk as children of light" (Eph. 5:8).

And again:

> "Ye are all the children of light and the children of the day" (1 Thess. 5:5).

Manifestly the lesson of these Scriptures is that the children of God, *i. e.,* they who are justified by faith through Jesus Christ, and who walk and live righteously, according to the nature imparted to them by their heavenly birth, are, Godward, as salt, causing the tolerance and forbearance of God toward the earth; and manward are as lights in the world bearing a testimony to the glory of their Father in heaven. (See Phil. 2:15, 16.)

Beyond any doubt, therefore, these words of the Lord apply directly to the saints of this age.

The Unity of the New Testament

One purpose that we have in mind in writing the foregoing pages is to exhibit the *unity of the theme of the New Testament.* That unity will be clearly perceived if we regard the Kingdom of heaven as the subject of both the Gospels and Epistles, and as being that new and *heavenly* realm (*in* the world but not *of* it), which the Son of God came down to earth to introduce, and which stands upon the foundation that was laid in His death and resurrection. In that view of the matter the Gospel of Matthew is seen to be in its rightful place as the Genesis of the New Testament; and John the Baptist is revealed in the *greatness* credited to him by the Lord's own testimony, as being—not the precursor merely of the earthly Kingdom promised to Israel, but—as *the herald of this present dispensation,* who came "in the spirit and power of Elijah"—not to announce the earthly Kingdom ("for the time of figs was not yet") but—"to turn the hearts of the fathers to the children, and the disobedient to the wisdom of the just, to make ready *a people prepared for the Lord"* (Luke 1:17). That prepared people undoubtedly is the "peculiar people" whom the Lord has redeemed from all iniquity and purified unto Himself (Titus 2:14). It is that "chosen generation," "royal priesthood," "holy nation," "peculiar people," which God has translated into the Kingdom of His dear Son, that they should "show forth the praises of Him Who has called them out of darkness into His marvellous light, who in time past were *not a people,* but *are now the people of God*" (1 Pet. 2:9, 10).

It is unspeakably satisfying to the heart to contemplate this unity and perfection of God's Word and work, instead of giving credence to a theory which introduces a violent break in the dealings of God through the ministry of His Son, assumes a complete change of purpose whereby the Church is substituted for the Kingdom, detaches John's message and ministry from this present age which it introduces, sets aside the Gospel of Matthew from its proper place, and postpones the direct application of the Lord's own words and commandments to a people yet unborn.

May the Lord give to all His peculiar people the seeing eye for the discerning of these things, and the submissive heart that rejoiceth in the doing of His will and that "delighteth greatly in His commandments."

Printed in the United States of America 2

P. WHITWELL WILSON *of the London Daily News*

The Christ We Forget

A Life of Our Lord for Men of To-day. 8vo, cloth, net $1.50.

A book with scarcely a peer in contemporary publishing. The author, an English University man, brilliant journalist, and sometime member of Parliament, writes the story of Jesus of Nazareth in a wonderfully arresting fashion. His book is utterly free from theological terminology or conventional viewpoint presenting a picture of Jesus which while actually new is astonishingly convincing.

EDGAR YOUNG MULLINS, D.D. *Pres. Southern Baptist Theo'l Sem., Louisville*

The Life in Christ Net $1.25.

"Dr. Mullins has recognition throughout the country as a great teacher. This volume shows him a preacher of intellectual and spiritual power. Excellent models for the growing minister, forcible, intellectual, spiritual."—*Christian Advocate.*

FRANCIS E. CLARK, D.D. *President United Society Christian Endeavor*

Christ and the Young People

12mo, cloth, net 50c.

"A study of the Life of Jesus in a quite unusual vein. The editor has seldom during his life been so helped by the printed page. It is indeed a remarkable presentation of the life of Jesus, sincere and impartial."—*Zion's Herald.*

JAMES M. GRAY, D.D. *Dean Moody Bible Institute*

A Picture of the Resurrection

12mo, boards, net 35c.

A plain, unadorned examination of the historical fact of Our Lord's Resurrection, of its indispensable prominence in the faith of the Christian and of the power its acceptance exercises in buttressing his belief in a physical resurrection from the dead, and the attainment of life eternal.

A. T. ROBERTSON, M.A., D.D.

The Divinity of Christ in the Gospel of John 12mo, cloth, net $1.00.

"A fascinating study of the Gospel of John. The book is not a full commentary on the Gospel, but an effort to develop the thesis of the book with brevity and clearness, so that the average man may understand the book better as a whole in detail."—*Christian Observer.*

QUESTIONS OF THE FAITH

LEWIS SPERRY CHAFER

The Kingdom in History and Prophecy

Introduction by C. I. Scofield. 12mo, cloth, net 75c.

"Anything that comes from the pen of this writer and Bible teacher may be accepted as thoroughly sound and intelligent in its presentation of truth. This is a study of the historical and prophetic aspects of the kingdom of God in their relations to the present age and that which is shortly to come."—*Christian Worker's Magazine.*

REV. D. M. CANRIGHT

The Complete Testimony

The Testimony of the Early Fathers, Proving the Universal Observance of Sunday in the First Centuries. 12mo, paper, net 20c.

The author of "Seventh Day Adventism" gives in concise, connected form the testimonies of all the early Christian Fathers from the Apostles down to A. D. 400. Invaluable to pastor and people—there is no other booklet like it.

C. F. WIMBERLY, B.A.

Behold the Morning!

The Imminent and Premillennial Coming of Jesus Christ. 12mo, cloth, net $1.15.

R. A. Torrey says: "I am sure the book will interest a great many in the subject, who have not been interested in the ordinary discussions of the subject. The book is one of the three books that I would recommend to any one who wishes to take up a study of the subject."

HENRY T. SELL, D.D.

Bible Studies in Vital Questions

12mo, cloth, net 60c; paper, net 35c.

The new volume of Sell's Bible Studies is prepared for adult Bible and pastors' classes and for use in schools, colleges and private study. It deals, in a plain, concise and constructive way, with the vital questions of the Christian faith about the Bible, God, Man and the Church. I. Vital Questions About the Bible. II. Vital Questions About God. III. Vital Questions About Man. IV. Vital Questions About the Church.

EDWARD LEIGH PELL

Author of "Pell's Notes on the Sunday School Lesson"

Our Troublesome Religious Questions

12mo, cloth, net $1.35.

A frank, earnest inquiry into, and discussion of, the problems of religious creed and conduct which vex and perplex believer and unbeliever alike. The author displays a marked ability to take up these questions and examine them with sagacity, impartiality and an optimistic, triumphant faith.

CPSIA information can be obtained
at www.ICGtesting.com
Printed in the USA
LVHW022144210523
747642LV00004B/35

9 781015 666863